Fruit of the Spirit: The Importance of Godly Character

Chris A. Legebow

DEDICATION

I dedicate this book to my Christian family: the Macchiavello family as I have witnessed true godly character in their lives. I thank God for His mercy towards me. I pray the book will help you expect transformation from glory to glory through the LORD Jesus Christ.

CONTENTS

ACKNOWLEDGMENTS

All scripture taken from Biblegateway.com
Modern English Version (MEV)

1 INTRODUCTION

Galatians 5: 22 But the fruit of the Spirit is love, joy, peace, patience, gentleness, goodness, faith, 23 meekness, and self-control; against such there is no law. 24 Those who are Christ's have crucified the flesh with its passions and lusts. 25 If we live in the Spirit, let us also walk in the Spirit. 26 Let us not be conceited, provoking one another and envying one another.

My book is a scriptural study on the fruit of the Holy Spirit. Jesus gave us the Holy Spirit as he promised he would do – contrast to fruit of flesh. After people are saved, especially after they have been baptized in the Holy Spirit, many people are interested in Spiritual gifts and their own personal gifts. The manifestations of the Holy Spirit are what equip us and empower us to witness Jesus Christ on the earth.

The Holy Spirit is a person. He has a distinct personality. He possesses all of the fruit of the Holy Spirit. He is the essence of those things. He is a person of the Trinity. He is God. His holy presence comes to live inside of Christians when they truly accept him as Saviour and Lord. His living inside of us brings a rebirth to our spirit.

All people were created in the image of God. They are triune: spirit, soul, body. The spirit part is there inside of every person but I would describe it as a shriveled up dry balloon. Once we accept Jesus Christ, God's Holy Spirit comes and fills the human spirit – like a balloon with air in it. With the new experience of being in direct communion with God, a person becomes more sensitive to God. The person will be lead or directed by the Holy Spirit who is dwelling inside of him or her.

John 3: 5 Jesus answered, "Truly, truly I say to you, unless a man is born of water and the Spirit, he cannot enter the kingdom of God. 6 That which is born of the flesh is flesh, and that which is born of the Spirit is spirit. 7 Do not marvel that I said to you, 'You must be born again.' 8 The wind blows where it wishes, and you hear its sound, but you do not know where it comes from or where it goes. So it is with everyone who is born of the Spirit."

With the spiritual rebirth or the indwelling of the Holy Spirit, the Holy Spirit directly teaches us things that are pleasing to God and things that are not. A person will receive a strong inner witness on the inside if something is not right. I would highly encourage all people to pray for the gift of discerning of spirits to come strong. If you are a new Christian or if you lead someone to Christ, pray for discerning of spirits. God can keep you from pits and snares by obedience to the inner prompting of the Holy Spirit.

Galatians 5: 16 I say then, walk in the Spirit, and you shall not fulfill the lust of the flesh. 17 For the flesh lusts against the Spirit, and the Spirit against the flesh. These are in opposition to one another, so that you may not do the things that you please. 18 But if you are led by the Spirit, you are not under the law.

The list of fruit of the flesh is not the focus of my book but they are mentioned as a contrast or the opposite of what God is like. Rather than the presence of God – they are the opposite. They are evil fruit from a fleshly or carnal soul.

Galatians 5: 19 Now the works of the flesh are revealed, which are these: adultery, sexual immorality, impurity, lewdness, 20 idolatry, sorcery, hatred, strife, jealousy, rage, selfishness, dissensions, heresies, 21 envy, murders, drunkenness, carousing, and the like. I warn you, as I previously warned you, that those who do such things shall not inherit the kingdom of God.

The origin of these fruit is the tree from the garden of Eden. The tree of the knowledge of Good and evil gave man knowledge of sin. Adam and Eve were forbidden to eat from its fruit. It never was God's desire for man to know evil. God only wanted us to know good. They were tempted of the devil who possessed the serpent and they took what changed their lives and all people who were born afterwards.

Genesis 3: 3 Now the serpent was more subtle than any beast of the field which the Lord God had made. And he said to the woman, "Has God said, 'You shall not eat of any tree of the garden'?"

2 And the woman said to the serpent, "We may eat of the fruit from the trees of the garden; 3 but from the fruit of the tree which is in the midst of the garden, God has said, 'You will not eat of it, nor will you touch it, or else you will die.' "4 Then the serpent said to the woman, "You surely will not die! 5 For God knows that on the day you eat of it your eyes will be opened and you will be like God, knowing good and evil."

6 When the woman saw that the tree was good for food, that it was pleasing to the eyes and a tree desirable to make one wise, she took of its fruit and ate; and she gave to her husband with her, and he ate. 7 Then the eyes of

both were opened, and they knew that they were naked. So they sewed fig leaves together and made coverings for themselves.

Man became aware of evil. They had enmity with God. They no longer had communion with God because they directly sinned by disobeying Him. Because of it, they lost their position in the earth. They could no longer live in the garden of Eden and had consequences of the curse of sin upon their lives. Man was sentenced to hard labour and woman to difficulty in bearing children and also that she would serve her husband. The origin of the fruit of the flesh is the tree of the knowledge of good and evil.

Once people become Christians, they no longer have to live in fleshly lusts or in the realms of the flesh. The person's spirit is reborn. And the person's communion with God is direct. God comes to live on the inside of each Christian giving direct access to God always. Sin has severe consequences and the most sever consequence is separation from God. God desires the best for all people but he will not force Himself on any person. Each person must of his or her own free will choose Jesus Christ as Saviour. It is unlike other religions because it is not merely a change of beliefs. The person of The Holy Spirit – God Himself – comes to dwell within the believer.

Jesus promised to send Holy Spirit

The disciples that were with Jesus enjoyed his presence. They had a unique spiritual relationship with him. They knew his character. They lived with him. They stayed with him. They were with Jesus for three years. They knew him more closely than all other people. When Jesus chose them it was more than for friendship. Jesus was choosing the people he most trusted to bring the good news of salvation or Messiah coming to all parts of the earth. It was through those disciples, we received the New Testament. It is through those disciples; the church was multiplied on the earth. He spoke to them explaining to them he would go to Jerusalem, die and rise from the dead on the third day. They did not understand he meant literally. He promised them something special. He promised them, and us, the person of the Holy Spirit. He promised to give them an indwelling presence who would give them peace and comfort. His words prophesied the coming of the Holy Spirit.

John 14: 25 "I have spoken these things to you while I am still with you. 26 But the Counselor, the Holy Spirit, whom the Father will send in My name, will teach you everything and remind you of all that I told you. 27 Peace I leave with you. My peace I give to you. Not as the world gives do I give to you. Let not your heart be troubled, neither let it be afraid.

After the sin of Adam, the Spirit of God would come upon his prophets and leaders. They knew and recognized God's presence and God used them. They did not know God the same way we do. The Holy Spirit lives within our spirit. The Holy Spirit's presence becomes one with us. We can know God intimately. Jesus promised it. The disciples didn't understand until after Christ had risen from the dead.

Receive the Holy Spirit

After Jesus rose from the dead, he appeared to his disciples and other believers for a period of 40 days. On one occasion as they were in the upper room that was locked. Jesus came in instantly – without coming through the door. He was in his glorified Body. He still had the nail prints in his hands and feet and the sword gash in his side. They knew and recognized him. He even ate with them. He spoke to them, and released the Holy Spirit to them before the day of Pentecost. As he talked with them, he breathed on them and said receive the Holy Spirit. It is similar to how God breathed life into Adam's body after he created him. The breath of God that imparts life.

John 20: 21 So Jesus said to them again, "Peace be with you. As My Father has sent Me, even so I send you." 22 When He had said this, He breathed on them and said to them, "Receive the Holy Spirit. 23 If you forgive the sins of anyone, they are forgiven them. If you retain the sins of anyone, they are retained."

After the 40 days on earth, Jesus was ascending up into heaven visibly with a crowd of more than 500 eye witnesses. Angels were around him. He had completed what He came to earth to do. He redeemed us. He taught us about the Holy Spirit. He now commanded the disciples to go and pray in Jerusalem so that they could be baptized in the Holy Spirit. They did not understand what it was. God was revealing new things to them. They only knew what He had taught them and what they were witnessing: the miracle of watching a person visibly ascend into heaven with angels around him. His instructions were his last words to them. They obeyed. 120 of them obeyed. They went to Jerusalem to the upper room and they prayed and waited for God to give them the promise of the Baptism of the Holy Spirit.

Acts 1: 4 Being assembled with them, He commanded them, "Do not depart from Jerusalem, but wait for the promise of the Father, of which you have heard from Me.[a] 5 For John baptized with water, but you shall be baptized with the Holy Spirit not many days from now."

Baptism of the Holy Spirit –

120 men and women gathered in the upper room. They were praying. They didn't know what it would result in. They had Jesus words. They didn't know how it would manifest the answer to their prayers. They were praying. They were obedient. Suddenly, the answer came. God's glorious presence filled the place. The Spirit of God came so strong that there was a strong wind even though they were inside a room. They began speaking in other tongues. They began praising God and worshipping God. Over their heads it appeared a unique experience; they could see something that has never been repeated – a manifest of glory of God upon each of them.

They were so moved by the Baptism of the Holy Spirit that it compelled them to go into the street below. They were still praising and worshipping God in other tongues. It wasn't a language they had learned or studied. It was God's presence using their mouths to speak other languages. There were pilgrims there who heard these men praising God in their native languages.

Acts 2: 2 When the day of Pentecost had come, they were all together in one place. 2 Suddenly a sound like a mighty rushing wind came from heaven, and it filled the whole house where they were sitting. 3 There appeared to them tongues as of fire, being distributed and resting on each of them, 4 and they were all filled with the Holy Spirit and began to speak in other tongues, as the Spirit enabled them to speak.

Some people believe they are drunk because they don't understand the tongues the people are speaking. Other know they are praising God in a different language. The Holy Spirit moves upon the Apostle Peter so that he recognizes "this is that". Peter has discerning of spirits really strong and realizes this is a fulfillment of prophesy of the prophet Joel where God promised to pour out his spirit on all people. The apostle gets boldness to speak and recognize the prophetic.

Acts 2: 14 But Peter, standing up with the eleven, lifted up his voice and said to them, "Men of Judea and all you who dwell in Jerusalem, let this be known to you, and listen to my words. 15 For these are not drunk, as you suppose, since it is the third hour of the day. 16 But this is what was spoken by the prophet Joel:

17 'In the last days it shall be,' says God,

'that I will pour out My Spirit on all flesh;
your sons and your daughters shall prophesy,
  your young men shall see visions,
  and your old men shall dream dreams.
18 Even on My menservants and maidservants
  I will pour out My Spirit in those days;
  and they shall prophesy.

Not only does Peter prophesy but he continues to preach how Jesus Christ came to the earth, suffered and died on the cross and rose from the dead to atone for all sin. The people are pilgrims, believers in Jehovah God. They gladly receive the evidence of the disciples speaking in tongues and their preaching on Jesus. They want to know how to receive Jesus. They want to be saved. Peter preaches the following words. The church multiplies instantly.

Acts 2: 38 Peter said to them, "Repent and be baptized, every one of you, in the name of Jesus Christ for the forgiveness of sins, and you shall receive the gift of the Holy Spirit. 39 For the promise is to you, and to your children, and to all who are far away, as many as the Lord our God will call."

40 With many other words he testified and exhorted them, saying, "Be saved from this perverse generation." 41 Then those who gladly received his word were baptized, and that day about three thousand souls were added to them.

Consistency is the power

The thousands of people had to be taught the things of God. They had to learn about the teachings of Jesus. They gathered together in homes each day to pray and to dine together. They cared for each other so that no one had nothing. They did go to the synagogue as usual, but they also met daily to learn about Jesus. The disciples of Jesus had to impart the things Jesus had taught them.

Acts 4: 32 All the believers were of one heart and one soul, and no one said that what he possessed was his own. But to them all things were in common. 33 With great power the apostles testified to the resurrection of the Lord Jesus, and great grace was on them all. 34 There was no one among them who lacked, for all those who were owners of land or houses sold them, and brought the income from what was sold, 35 and placed it at the apostles' feet. And it was distributed to each according to his need.

They had been empowered by the Holy Spirit to do it. The baptism of the Holy Spirit empowers a person for service, with gifts of the Spirit but also, the Baptism of the Holy Spirit allows direct communion with God spirit to Spirit. Praying in the Holy Spirit, allows God to pray in us, and through us, the perfect will of God for us.

Romans 8: 26 Likewise, the Spirit helps us in our weaknesses, for we do not know what to pray for as we ought, but the Spirit Himself intercedes for us with groanings too deep for words. 27 He who searches the hearts knows what the mind of the Spirit is, because He intercedes for the saints according to the will of God.

Consistency

Read the scripture, pray always, keep worshipping God.

Upon entrance to the promised land – first promised to Abraham, Isaac and Jacob made Israel, God spoke to encourage Joshua in his leadership of Israel into the new experience. They were entering the promised land. They were no longer in slavery. They were no longer in the wilderness. They were coming to the place of inheriting their promises. God emphasized the importance of the commandments. God emphasized the importance of reading the word daily, confessing it, praying it, posting it in every place so that it would remind the people of what he had done for them. God emphasized the Word of God had to be in the hearts of the people.

The disciples of Jesus in the early church were teaching the scriptures. They were explaining how Jesus fulfilled all Messianic prophecy and they were sharing about the miracles that Jesus had done. Similar to Joshua bringing the people into a new experience, they were launching the church that would be multiplied throughout the earth.

Joshua 1 : 7 Be strong and very courageous, in order to act carefully in accordance with all the law that My servant Moses commanded you. Do not turn aside from it to the right or the left, so that you may succeed wherever you go. 8 This Book of the Law must not depart from your mouth. Meditate on it day and night so that you may act carefully according to all that is written in it. For then you will make your way successful, and you will be wise. 9 Have not I commanded you? Be strong and courageous. Do not be afraid or dismayed, for the Lord your God is with you wherever you go."

The apostle Paul did not know Jesus as he lived on the earth but he encountered Jesus while he was on the road to Damascus. He was a murderer of Christians until that day. He met Jesus and his life was completely changed. He immediately believed in Jesus Christ. He knew he had encountered God. He obeyed instruction and waited until Ananias came and laid hands on him to bring healing to him. He had been blinded by the bright light of God's presence.

Acts 9: 5 He said, "Who are You, Lord?"

The Lord said, "I am Jesus, whom you are persecuting. It is hard for you to kick against the goads." 6 Trembling and astonished, he said, "Lord, what will You have me do?" The Lord said to him, "Rise up and go into the city, and you will be told what you must do."

The Apostle Paul, immediately started preaching and teaching Jesus Christ. It transformed His life. He was water baptized and baptized in the Holy Spirit. He preached Jesus throughout the realms of Israel but also Europe. He knew Jesus and taught the truths of God and wrote a large part of our New Testament. In these words, he encourages the Church to keep rejoicing and praying and giving thanks. He warns them not to grieve the Holy Spirit. The Holy Spirit is a person.

1 Thessalonians 5: 16 Rejoice always. 17 Pray without ceasing. 18 In everything give thanks, for this is the will of God in Christ Jesus concerning you.

19 Do not quench the Spirit.

Holy Spirit will lead us, guide us, correct us

So the baptism of the Holy Spirit is to empower us to share Christ throughout the earth in all spheres of our authority. Also though, by communing with the Holy Spirit in prayer in tongues, we built up our spirit man. What that means is just like an athlete build up his body so he can function at optimum ability, a Christian can build up his or her spirit so that the Holy Spirit transforms us. The more Christians are in God's presence, the more Christ transforms us. It is His living presence that transforms our character to be more Christlike. It never comes against our will.

What God will do is show us areas by the prompting of the Holy Spirit, that are pleasing to Him; He will also show us areas, where we need to change. It will grieve the Holy Spirit within us and we will know it is not right. We can repent and read the word of God about that thing and memorize the word and pray the word and speak or confess it over our lives. The Holy Spirit will remind us of the things that God has taught us. The Holy Spirit quickens scriptures to you so you can speak them to others or so that you can apply them in your own life.

John 14: 26 But the Counselor, the Holy Spirit, whom the Father will send in My name, will teach you everything and remind you of all that I told you. 27 Peace I leave with you. My peace I give to you. Not as the world gives do I give to you. Let not your heart be troubled, neither let it be afraid.

Character of Christ – being like God – letting the Holy Spirit use you for the glory of God

Consistency in prayer, praise, worship, reading of scripture is the way that God chooses to transform us. It is our active seeking or pursuing of God that He transforms us. It can occur while we are reading the word of God. It can occur while we are praying. It can occur while we are praising God. It occurs while we are desiring to worship God with all our being – God's Holy Spirit transforms us beyond what we were. It is as though a spirit of growth, a eureka moment or a revelation that comes. The person will suddenly realize growth in an area of life. It is the Holy Spirit who does it. We can in no way do it ourselves. It is the manifest presence of God that does it.

2 Corinthians 3: 18 But we all, seeing the glory of the Lord with unveiled faces, as in a mirror, are being transformed into the same image from glory to glory by the Spirit of the Lord.

Jesus promised to send the Holy Spirit. Jesus promised that the Holy Spirit would teach us about Jesus Christ. The Holy Spirit teaches us, and transforms us. The Holy Spirit can show us things in the future. The Holy Spirit becomes our direct teacher. As those early disciples gathered daily to learn about God, we can commune with God each day learning more about Him. The Holy Spirit directly teaches us. Pastor Yonggi Chou of Korea has a book on the topic of The Holy Spirit my senior Partner. He is known for the largest church with more than 100, 000 members.

The book taught the importance of relying on the Holy Spirit to take the lead in daily decisions as well as in major decisions. He explains how it helped him in ministry but also in acquiring church buildings and practical areas of business.

John 16: 7 Nevertheless I tell you the truth: It is expedient for you that I go away. For if I do not go away, the Counselor will not come to you. But if I go, I will send Him to you. 8 When He comes, He will convict the world of sin and of righteousness and of judgment: 9 of sin, because they do not believe in Me; 10 of righteousness, because I am going to My Father, and you will see Me no more; 11 and of judgment, because the ruler of this world stands condemned.

John 16: 13 But when the Spirit of truth comes, He will guide you into all truth. For He will not speak on His own authority. But He will speak whatever He hears, and He will tell you things that are to come. 14 He will glorify Me, for He will receive from Me and will declare it to you. 15 All that the Father has is Mine. Therefore, I said that He will take what is Mine and will declare it to you.

The truth is that once you come to know Jesus Christ, you are bearing fruit already. Before you are a Christian, you've got some experience from life; you've got some personality traits; you've got character strengths; you've got areas that require improvement. Not many people know the areas they can improve in. Usually if a person tells them, they are insulted. No one wants to receive news telling them to change their inner most being. The Holy Spirit can come in such a way that with a gentle nudging, like the softest brush of a breeze, the Holy Spirit can reveal to us areas to change; more than that though, He never reveals to us unless we are in the midst of transformation. The Holy Spirit living in us not only shows us but also transforms us as He is teaching us.

A tree is known by its fruit

The evidence of a tree is in its fruit. This simple but profound truth is evident in each of us as well as in the trees. The type of fruit being formed reveal the type of tree; apples grown on apple trees; pears grow on pear tresses; cherries grow on cherry trees. Godly fruit grows in the life of someone wholly yielding to the Holy Spirit. Godly fruit is evident in the fruit that Galatians describes.

A person's fruit is witnessed by his or her words: what he or she talks about and how he or she talks about it. A person's fruit is evident in life choices he or she makes – choosing God's way or choosing a different way. A person's fruit is evident in the general character or countenance of a person whether or not he or she is joyful.

Luke 6: 43 "A good tree does not bear corrupt fruit, nor does a corrupt tree bear good fruit. 44 Each tree is known by its own fruit. Men do not gather figs from thorns, nor do they gather grapes from a wild bush. 45 A good man out of the good treasure of his heart bears what is good, and an evil man out of the evil treasure of his heart bears what is evil. For of the abundance of the heart his mouth speaks.

Matthew 12: 33 "Either make the tree good and its fruit good, or else make the tree corrupt and its fruit corrupt. For the tree is known by its fruit. 34 O generation of vipers, how can you, being evil, speak good things? For out of the abundance of the heart the mouth speaks. 35 A good man out of the good treasure of his heart brings forth good things. And an evil man out of the evil treasure brings forth evil things. 36 But I say to you that for every idle word that men speak, they will give an account on the Day of Judgment. 37 For by your words you will be justified, and by your words you will be condemned."

In my book I will examine the characteristics of the fruit of the Spirit as through the scriptures.

love
 joy,
peace,
patience, forbearance
gentleness, meekness
goodness,
faith,
self-control;

2 LOVE

Knowing the love of God is beyond what can be explained in language but it is important to share different aspects of it so that you might know there are depths to it and heights of it that have not yet been experienced. Because God is eternal, because He is the essence of love itself, humans cannot comprehend it. I remember going to the beach as a child and seeing how huge the lake seemed. It was Lake Erie and you cannot see the other side of it. It was awesome. Although I was much older, my first view of the Pacific Coast was similar. The water goes on and on.

People from outside of our region don't understand our reliance on the lakes. In the same way as the ocean goes on and on for miles, God's love is unmeasurable. In this chapter, I will give you glimpses of God's love. I will explain it as a multi-sided huge crystal chandelier or disco ball that has many sides to it so light is projected in diverse ways. Each person's view of it is slightly different although there is only one God. People experience God's love in different ways as well.

Kinds of love known to those in the New Testament included Philia which is brotherly love, Eros which is passionate love and agape, the God kind that is unconditional and vast. Most people understand brotherly love is different that Eros. To understand Agape, you must experience it yourself. It's the type of love that only God can give. God is the source. God is the giver of it and through experiencing His divine love, we also can give it and be vessels filled with it.

Even as Adam and Eve sinned and were judged by God, God had the prophetic word about the Messiah who would come and redeem mankind thousands of years later. God spoke that the seed of woman would be born to crush the serpent's head. Jesus, the Messiah would be born to die for our sins so that we could be in communion with God. I'm not sure you understand how profound the idea is – the same God pronouncing judgement most serious and horrible also says – but I will send someone who will come and die for you so that you may be saved.

15 I will put enmity
    between you and the woman,
    and between your offspring and her offspring;
he will bruise your head,
    and you will bruise his heel."
God's mercy towards man – plan of a Messiah before the birth of the first

child – Genesis
The God kind of love – unconditional John 3: 16
Mercy towards Noah
Chance for life for Noah's family and the animals.
Promise it would not occur again

In a different passage, it tells us that God knew us and made provision for us before the foundation of the world.

Ephesians 1: 4 just as He chose us in Him before the foundation of the world, to be holy and blameless before Him in love; 5 He predestined us to adoption as sons to Himself through Jesus Christ according to the good pleasure of His will, 6 to the praise of the glory of His grace which He graciously bestowed on us in the Beloved.

There is nothing that you or I can do to get God to love us more. He has already shown us His love by sending Christ. God loved us because He created us for His glory. If you have ever created a painting or a poem or something, you feel some certain love towards that thing. Parents of children often stare at their child with amazement knowing that part of them in in the child and they are amazed at simple things the child does such as smile or utter a sound. It is a fraction of the kind of passion feels towards us. He sent Jesus Christ to be born of the Virgin Mary. Jesus lived as a man and learned a trade and worked with his dad until he was 30 years old. Jesus knew he had come to the earth to give his life – to be a sacrifice – for all the sins of all people who would ever live.

John 3: 16 "For God so loved the world that He gave His only begotten Son, that whoever believes in Him should not perish, but have eternal life. 17 For God did not send His Son into the world to condemn the world, but that the world through Him might be saved.

Although he committed no sin against God or man, he was sentenced to die because he proclaimed he was the Messiah. He was crucified, died and was buried and rose from the dead on the 3rd day. He was on earth for forty days and then ascended into heaven visibly before 500 witnesses. The angels with him proclaimed that Jesus would return as He promised. It is for his second coming that true Christians are expecting Him to come.

Noah

God reached out to Noah hundreds of years after Adam and Eve. The people were very wicked but Noah was different; something in him worshipped God. Through Noah's life God witnesses for 120 years to the people of his generation. Noah built a huge ark and he and his family and the animals that came in the ark were saved. God kept his promise to Noah and set a rainbow as a symbol of His covenant that never again would he destroy the earth with a flood.

Genesis 6: 8 But Noah found grace in the eyes of the Lord.

Genesis 9: 12 Then God said, "This is the sign of the covenant which I am making between Me and you and every living creature that is with you, for all future generations. 13 I have set My rainbow in the cloud, and it shall be a sign of a covenant between Me and the earth.

Abraham

Abraham was living in the midst of idol worshippers but he was different. He truly desired to know God and God revealed himself to him in such a way that Abraham left all his family, except his nephew who insisted on coming, to go where God said He would lead him. He was prosperous; he was established; he could have lived in UR of the Chaldees and been happy, but God called him out of all that he knew and promised to make him a heritage as vast as the stars in the sky and as grains of sand on a beach. Although Abraham had no children and he and his wife were in their 70's, God promised them children, so many children they couldn't count them all. That's a pretty amazing promise. What faith it must have taken to leave all he knew to go to no destination – but to obey God wholly and let God lead him to the land he promised.

God spoke with Abraham repeatedly and Abraham obeyed God. Abraham inherited the land, became prosperous and got to know God in a special way.

Genesis 12: I will make of you a great nation;
   I will bless you
and make your name great,
   so that you will be a blessing.
3 I will bless them who bless you
   and curse him who curses you,[a]
and in you all families of the earth
   will be blessed."

Genesis 13: 15 All the land that you see I will give to you and to your descendants forever. 16 I will make your descendants like the dust of the earth, so that if a man could number the dust of the earth, then your descendants could also be numbered. 17 Arise, and walk throughout the land across its length and its width, for I will give it to you."

Genesis 26: 2 The Lord appeared to him and said, "Do not go down to Egypt. Live in the land of which I will tell you. 3 Sojourn in this land, and I will be with you and will bless you; for I will give to you and all your descendants all these lands, and I will fulfill the oath which I swore to Abraham your father. 4 I will make your descendants multiply as the stars of the heavens and will give your descendants all these lands. By your descendants all the nations of the earth will be blessed,[a] 5 because Abraham obeyed Me and kept My charge, My commandments, My statutes, and My laws."

God's love is evident in these covenants that he made with people. He was reaching out towards us so that there could be a holy people in the earth. He kept his word to Abraham. Abraham had children while he was nearly a 100 years old. Through him came Isaac; Isaac had Jacob. Through Jacob transformed, he was called Israel. Israel had 12 sons who are the them the foundations of the nation Israel.

Through the nation of Israel God has preserved the Word of God given to Moses. Through the nation of Israel, God has shown us His exceeding mercies because even though Israel stopped worshipping God and turned to idols, God forgave them when they repented and after thousands of years, He gave them the land of Israel once more and gathered them and is gathering them from all the places where they had been scattered.

Psalm 147: The Lord builds up Jerusalem;
    He gathers together the outcasts of Israel.

Isaiah 11: 12 He shall set up a banner for the nations,
    and shall assemble the outcasts of Israel,
and gather together the dispersed of Judah
    from the four corners of the earth.

Moses

God chose Moses to lead Israel out of Egyptian bondage for 400 years. Through miracles that affected all of Egypt, the Pharaoh's heart was softened to let Moses and Israel go free. By God's authority, Moses stretched out his staff over the Red Sea and it parted.

Exodus 14: 21 Then Moses stretched out his hand over the sea, and the Lord caused the sea to go back by a strong east wind all that night, and made the sea dry land, so that the waters were divided. 22 The children of Israel went into the midst of the sea on the dry ground, and the waters were a wall unto them on their right hand, and on their left.

Moses lead them through the wilderness of Sanai. God provided shade and light for them. God provided manna or bread for them and water in the midst of a desert – from out of a rock. At Mount Sinai, there they received the commandments of God. Moses read them to the people. It was God's Covenant with Israel. They would keep his laws and they would be His people. He would bless them and prosper them.

Deuteronomy 5: 32 Therefore, be careful to do as the Lord your God has commanded you. You shall not turn aside to the right hand or to the left. 33 You shall walk in all the ways which the Lord your God has commanded you, so that you may live and that it may be well with you, and that you may prolong your days in the land which you shall possess.

Deuteronomy 30: 9 The Lord your God will make you prosper in every work of your hand, in the offspring of your body, and in the offspring of your livestock, and in the produce of your land, for good. For the Lord will once again rejoice over you for good, just as He rejoiced over your fathers, 10 if you obey the voice of the Lord your God, by keeping His commandments and His statutes which are written in this Book of the Law, and if you return to the Lord your God with all your heart and with all your soul.

God taught Israel

God gave Moses 613 Levitical laws. God instructed Moses to establish Aaron's family as priests who wholly lived their lives unto God. God taught Moses and gave him detailed instruction about how to create a dwelling place for the presence of God. God was going to live in their midst – the glory of God would be there so they would have his protection.

Exodus 25: 17 You shall make a mercy seat of pure gold, two and a half cubits long and one and a half cubits wide. 18 You shall make two cherubim of gold, make them of hammered work at the two ends of the mercy seat. 19 Make one cherub on the one end and the other cherub on the other end. From the mercy seat you shall make the cherubim on its two ends. 20 The cherubim shall stretch forth their wings upward, covering the mercy seat with their wings and facing one another. The faces of the cherubim are to face toward the mercy seat. 21 You shall put the mercy seat above upon the ark, and in the ark you shall put the testimony that I will give you. 22 I will meet with you there, and I will meet with you from above the mercy seat, from between the two cherubim which are upon the ark of the testimony. I will speak with you all that I will command you for the children of Israel.

Mosaic covenant – God's teaching us His ways and His will

Moses wrote all of the Torah (Genesis, Exodus, Leviticus, Numbers, and Deuteronomy). It was the first that God gave scripture to man. God gave us His own words to live by and to learn from. It was God's direct way of communicating how we should live our lives. God's word shows us what is pleasing to God and warns us of the things we must not do. God's Word applies to every area of our lives. It was the foundation of our laws in North America. Obedience to God's Word positions people to live a prosperous, successful, abundant life.

Joshua

Joshua was chosen by God to follow Moses and God promised He would keep his covenant as he did with Moses. He made it clear that the Word of God was the priority. They were to be a Holy people, set apart unto God. God would give them the land promised to Abraham keeping his covenant with Abraham through Israel, his descendants.

Joshua 1: 7 Be strong and very courageous, in order to act carefully in accordance with all the law that My servant Moses commanded you. Do not turn aside from it to the right or the left, so that you may succeed wherever you go. 8 This Book of the Law must not depart from your mouth. Meditate on it day and night so that you may act carefully according to all that is written in it. For then you will make your way successful, and you will be wise.

Joshua lead Israel through all of the land that God had promised to them. They fought but God gave them the strategy and the victory. All of the 12 tribes of Israel inherited the land they were promised – as promised through Abraham.

Joshua 23: 3 You have seen all that the Lord your God did to all these peoples before you, for it is the Lord your God who has waged war for you. 4 See, I have allotted to you as an inheritance the land of these peoples who remain, along with the land of the peoples whom I defeated, from the Jordan to the Mediterranean Sea in the west. 5 The Lord your God will drive them out and dispossess them from before you, and you will inherit their land, as the Lord your God told you.

Holy Scripture

These covenants above are slices of God's mercy and love towards us is shown through His continual making of covenants with us throughout the years. He drew us to Himself by His mercy towards us. He entrusted men (also women) of God with His Words to us. Finally, established were the words of God in scripture. He used other prophets and apostles to write scripture. It is through the Scriptures, a believer can receive insight and wisdom. It is by studying the Word of God and living it that we become more like Christ. God draws us by His Holy Spirit so that we may know Him. God promised that He would not only give us scripture but that His words would be written in our hearts so that we would desire to live in His ways.

God not only gave us the Scriptures, but as we read them prayerfully they become engrafted into our hearts – written in the inward parts of us so that we align with God's Word. We begin to think according to scripture and live according to scripture as well as make decisions with God's Word at the standard. It means we can live a life pleasing to God; we can have totally communion with God.

Jeremiah 31: 33 But this shall be the covenant that I will make with the house of Israel
    after those days, says the Lord:
I will put My law within them
    and write it in their hearts;
and I will be their God,
    and they shall be My people

Ezekiel 11: 19 I will give them one heart, and I will put a new spirit within them. And I will take the stony heart out of their flesh, and give them a heart of flesh, 20 that they may walk in My statutes, and keep My ordinances, and do them. And they shall be My people, and I will be their God.

Jesus Christ – Messiah – living it – living word

Jesus message to the people was a message of life, hope and peace.

He announced his ministry in the synagogue after he read the scripture.

Isaiah 61: 1 The Spirit of the Lord God is upon me
   because the Lord has anointed me
   to preach good news to the poor;
He has sent me to heal the broken-hearted,
   to proclaim liberty to the captives,
   and the opening of the prison to those who are bound;
2 to proclaim the acceptable year of the Lord
   and the day of vengeance of our God;
to comfort all who mourn,
3   to preserve those who mourn in Zion,
to give to them beauty
   for ashes,
the oil of joy
   for mourning,
the garment of praise
   for the spirit of heaviness,
that they might be called trees of righteousness,
   the planting of the Lord,
   that He might be glorified.

The message was of salvation, healing and deliverance that only the Messiah could fulfill. Jesus proclaimed it was written of him. The Pharisees wanted to kill him for saying it. For 3 years, Jesus demonstrated the words he read by bringing hope to the people of salvation and freedom from sin; he healed the sick; he raised the dead; he cast out demons. Often the term used to describe Jesus was his compassion.

Moved with compassion to heal

During his preaching and teaching, people would be healed or delivered of demons. A large gathering of people began to crowd around him wherever he went. He would go into the country so that there would a large free space for people to gather. His message was the good news or gospel that Messiah had come so people could be free from all sin and the curse of sin.

Matthew 14: 14 Jesus went ashore and saw a great assembly. And He was moved with compassion toward them, and He healed their sick.

Jesus made it clear that it was God's will to heal people. The leper had faith that if Jesus would do it, he could be healed. Jesus met him at his point of faith and gave the word that he was willing to heal him. He commanded him to be clean or be whole of his leprosy.

Healing of the leper

Mark 1: 40 A leper came to Him, pleading with Him and kneeling before Him, saying, "If You are willing, You can make me clean."

41 Then Jesus, moved with compassion, extended His hand and touched him, and said to him, "I will. Be clean." 42 As soon as He had spoken, the leprosy immediately departed from him, and he was cleansed.

Preached good news – did miracles, healed people, promised the Holy Spirit

All during his ministry, Jesus preached to all types of people. He was a favourite of common people because he taught them in parables. God's word clearly says that Jesus went about doing good. It was not God's will that people be in sin or bondage.

Acts 10: 38 how God anointed Jesus of Nazareth with the Holy Spirit and with power, who went about doing good and healing all who were oppressed by the devil, for God was with Him.

A new commandment

Jesus gave a new commandment. His commandment was that people would love each other with the same love He loved them with. It sounds simple but Jesus loved the people unconditionally. Jesus had the agape kind of love so that He saw the best qualities in each person. He spoke of what he himself would do – to lay down his life for a friend. Literally he died for us so that we could be restored back to God.

John 15: 11 I have spoken these things to you, that My joy may remain in you, and that your joy may be full. 12 This is My commandment: that you love one another, as I have loved you. 13 Greater love has no man than this: that a man lay down his life for his friends.

The only way that people can love each other with agape love is to first receive it from Christ. If we receive the forgiveness of sins, the communion with God that Jesus gave us, we will know love that is unconditional and passionate. God loves us as his own children. His love towards us is overwhelming. By being in God's holy presence, our inner man is transformed so that we also not only receive the agape love but are moved with mercy or empathy towards people and animals. We begin to care for life because we know the creator in an intimate way.

Jesus to the rich young ruler

Jesus called 12 disciples. The rich young ruler who desired the secret to eternal life came but his heart was not seeking God truly as he enjoyed his position and his money. He said he had kept all the commandments. First of all, it is highly unlikely that anyone could do it. It was as though the rich young ruler wanted something beyond what was written by Moses – some inner truth more profound that God's Word. Jesus did not ask any other person he called into ministry to go sell everything and give to the poor.

Jesus was showing the ruler what the secret to eternal life was – loving God with all your heart, your soul, your mind and your strength. Loving God more than anything is the whole foundation of Judaism and also Christianity. The ruler realized how much wealth and power he had. He did not want to obey Jesus invitation to sell all and follow Jesus. Notice verse 21. Jesus saw him; Jesus knew him and that he loved money more than anything; Jesus loved him. Even though he knew the ruler would not follow him, Jesus loved him.

Mark 10: 17 When He set out on His way, a man came running and knelt before Him, and asked Him, "Good Teacher, what must I do to inherit eternal life?"

18 He said to him, "Why do you call Me good? No one is good, except God alone. 19 You know the commandments, Do not commit adultery, Do not murder, Do not steal, Do not bear false witness, Do not defraud, Honor your father and mother.[c]"

20 He answered Him, "Teacher, all these have I observed from my youth."

21 Then Jesus, looking upon him, loved him and said to him, "You lack one thing: Go your way, sell whatever you have and give to the poor, and you will have treasure in heaven. And come, take up the cross and follow Me."

22 He was saddened by that word, and he went away grieving. For he had many possessions.

Promise of return

Jesus love towards Peter

Jesus knew that Peter would deny knowing him. Jesus dined with him and loved him. He prophesied to him that he would do it.

Mark 14: 30 Jesus said to him, "Truly, I say to you that this day, during the night, before the rooster crows twice, you will deny Me three times."

This was only several hours before Jesus was going to be arrested. Jesus knew but in spite of the disciples' character flaws, and conditional love, Jesus loved them. The following passage is the account of Jesus arrest and sentencing while Peter stood without the temple. It details his denying of Jesus.

Luke 22: 54 Then they arrested Him, and led Him away, and brought Him into the high priest's house. Peter followed at a distance. 55 But when they had kindled a fire in the middle of the courtyard and sat down together, Peter sat among them. 56 Then a servant girl saw him as he sat near the fire, and gazed at him, and said, "This man was with Him."

57 But he denied Him, saying, "Woman, I do not know Him."

58 A little later someone else saw him and said, "You also are one of them."

Peter said, "Man, I am not!"

59 About an hour later another man firmly declared, "Certainly, this man also was with Him, for he is a Galilean."

60 Peter said, "Man, I do not know what you are saying." Immediately, while he was yet speaking, the rooster crowed. 61 The Lord turned and looked at Peter. Then Peter remembered the word of the Lord, how He had told him, "Before the rooster crows, you will deny Me three times." 62 And Peter went outside and wept bitterly.

None of the other disciples stayed with him during his trial at the Sanhedrin. John was present but silently. Peter realized what Jesus had prophesied over him had come true. I'm sure Peter must have had a sense of being a traitor. After all. He had lived with Jesus and had seen him do the miracles for 3 years.

In the scriptures to say something repeatedly is verification of it. Saying thrice, meant that it was like a divorce from the person. Peter had divorced himself from association with Jesus, while only several hours previous he had begged Jesus to wash his hands and his head because Jesus said if he didn't wash their feet, they could have no place in him. Peter was all in with Jesus until Jesus was arrested.

Special care to restore him

Upon Jesus Resurrection, Jesus purposely appeals to Peter. He appears to them at the Sea of Tiberias. Jesus especially cooks them dinner and speaks with them as a group. He has a special question for Peter. Peter says yes. The pattern occurs 3 times, so that three times, Peter says he loves Jesus. This is a special way of Peter confirming his alignment with Jesus once more. It is not mere coincidence. It is Jesus way of healing Peter from any hatred of himself for being a coward when he denied Christ. It is a healing for Peter to affirm his love for Christ. It is also instructional. Jesus calls Peter to go preach and care for God's lambs and sheep. He prophesies about Peter's future of being martyred for his faith. It is a confirmation of the calling to be a disciple and a release into ministry by Jesus Himself.

John 21: 15 So when they had eaten breakfast, Jesus said to Simon Peter, "Simon, son of John, do you love Me more than these?"

He said to Him, "Yes, Lord. You know that I love You."

He said to him, "Feed My lambs."

16 He said to him again a second time, "Simon, son of John, do you love Me?"

He said to Him, "Yes, Lord. You know that I love You."

He said to him, "Tend My sheep."

17 He said to him the third time, "Simon, son of John, do you love Me?"

Peter was grieved because He asked him the third time, "Do you love Me?" He said to Him, "Lord, You know everything. You know that I love You."

Jesus said to him, "Feed My sheep. 18 Truly, truly I say to you, when you were young, you dressed yourself and walked where you desired. But when you are old, you will stretch out your hands, and another will dress you and carry you where you do not want to go." 19 He said this, signifying by what kind of death he would glorify God. When He had said this, He said to him, "Follow Me."

Jesus commission to preach to all people so that all people could be saved.

Jesus prayer request

There is only one prayer request of Jesus recorded in the Bible and it is that God would release more people to preach and teach Christ. During his life Jesus commissioned the 12 to go about saving, healing and delivering and doing good works for the kingdom of God. Later, he anoints the 70 and releases them to go preach and teach Jesus, to save, to heal to deliver. Jesus was calling disciples while he was on the earth. It is Jesus' desire that all people would know that if they would believe on him, they could be saved. It is the agape love of God that compelled him to release other labourers.

It is that same compassion that comes upon Apostles, prophets, Evangelists, pastors and teachers. It is the same compassion that comes upon any Christian who shares his or her testimony or witnesses Christ to a stranger or to a friend. It is the agape love of God that compels Christians to preach and teach or give to those who do. It is why Christians are involved in missions caring for people in different countries. It is the agape love of God.

Matthew 9: 35 Jesus went throughout all the cities and villages, teaching in their synagogues, preaching the gospel of the kingdom, and healing every sickness and every disease among the people. 36 But when He saw the crowds, He was moved with compassion for them, because they fainted and were scattered, like sheep without a shepherd. 37 Then He said to His disciples, "The harvest truly is plentiful, but the laborers are few. 38 Therefore, pray to the Lord of the harvest, that He will send out laborers into His harvest."

Luke 10: 10 After this the Lord appointed seventy others, and sent them two by two ahead of Him into every city and place where He Himself was about to come. 2 He said to them, "The harvest truly is plentiful, but the laborers are few. Pray therefore the Lord of the harvest to send out laborers into His harvest.

The Resurrection

After the resurrection of Jesus from the dead, Jesus commissions those gathered around him including the 12 disciples, to preach the good news of salvation through Jesus Christ. He commissions them to go into "all of the world". He literally means all people groups, every people, every tribe, every nation. He commissions them by speaking a word of release over them or a word giving them authority to preach and teach with salvations, healing, deliverance as signs of their authority. It is the same word that applies to all believers in Jesus that we should share Christ's good news with all people groups until Jesus returns.

Mark 16: 15 He said to them, "Go into all the world, and preach the gospel to every creature. 16 He who believes and is baptized will be saved. But he who does not believe will be condemned. 17 These signs will accompany those who believe: In My name they will cast out demons; they will speak with new tongues; 18 they will take up serpents; if they drink any deadly thing, it will not hurt them; they will lay hands on the sick, and they will recover."

Matthew 28: 18 Then Jesus came and spoke to them, saying, "All authority has been given to Me in heaven and on earth. 19 Go therefore and make disciples of all nations, baptizing them in the name of the Father and of the Son and of the Holy Spirit, 20 teaching them to observe all things I have commanded you. And remember, I am with you always, even to the end of the age." Amen.

Believe on the Lord Jesus and be saved

The gift of eternal life, of forgiveness of sins and of communion with God is a gift of ultimate love. It is simple. It is so simple, people do not accept it. They must believe it and confess it with their mouth that Jesus died for their sins, so they could be saved. The scripture instructs us clearly what is required of a Christian. His mercy towards us is such that should we believe and receive Jesus, we are made Holy by his blood shed for us. We can be in intimate relationship with God. The heart of the good news of the gospel is love. It is God's unconditional agape love for us.

Romans 10: 8 But what does it say? "The word is near you, in your mouth and in your heart."[d] This is the word of faith that we preach: 9 that if you confess with your mouth Jesus is Lord, and believe in your heart that God has raised Him from the dead, you will be saved, 10 for with the heart one believes unto righteousness, and with the mouth confession is made unto salvation. 11 For the Scripture says, "Whoever believes in Him will not be ashamed."[e] 12 For there is no distinction between Jew and Greek, for the same Lord over all is generous toward all who call upon Him. 13 For, "Everyone who calls on the name of the Lord shall be saved."[f]

John 3: 16 "For God so loved the world that He gave His only begotten Son, that whoever believes in Him should not perish, but have eternal life. 17 For God did not send His Son into the world to condemn the world, but that the world through Him might be saved.

God's mercy evident in His consistent reaching towards us and giving us mercy – through the blood of Jesus

Jesus blessed the children

Jesus showed special love for certain groups of people who were often neglected or not given prominence in their society. One of those groups is the children. People wanted the best for their children. They believed God's word that the laying on of hands could impart a blessing. They were bringing the most special people to them to Jesus, their children. Jesus disciples thought they would screen the people who got close to Jesus and they tried to stop the children from coming to Jesus. Jesus corrected them. He called the children unto himself and blessed them. Jesus showed humble love in caring for those who could give him nothing but their hearts.

Mark 10: 13 They brought young children to Him, that He might touch them. But the disciples rebuked those who brought them. 14 But when Jesus saw it, He was very displeased and said to them, "Allow the little children to come to Me, and do not forbid them, for of such is the kingdom of God. 15 Truly I say to you, whoever does not receive the kingdom of God as a little child shall not enter it." 16 And He took them up in His arms, put His hands on them, and blessed them.

Jesus mercy towards woman caught in adultery

Jesus showed special mercy for women. He cast demons out of Mary Magdalene and she followed him to get teachings from him. There were other women who had money that helped give to Jesus ministry. His mercy and compassion shown to the woman caught in adultery is possibly the one excerpt from scripture that summarizes his love for all of us. A woman or man caught in adultery should clearly be stoned to death according to the law of Moses. If the woman was caught in the act of adultery – there must have been a man there also, yet only the woman was brought to judgement. Their society was prejudiced against women and especially a sinner. The Pharisees hoped to catch Jesus in disobeying the laws of Moses because they knew he preached a message of love.

John 8: 8 But Jesus went to the Mount of Olives. 2 Early in the morning He returned to the temple. All the people came to Him, and He sat down and taught them. 3 The scribes and Pharisees brought a woman caught in adultery. When they had put her in the middle, 4 they said to Him, "Teacher, this woman was caught in the very act of adultery. 5 Now Moses in the law commanded us to stone such, but what do You say?" 6 They said this, testing Him, that they might have something of which to accuse Him.
But Jesus stooped down and wrote on the ground with His finger, as though He did not hear them. 7 So when they continued asking Him, He stood up and said to them, "Let him who is without sin among you be the first to throw a stone at her." 8 Again He stooped down and wrote on the ground.

No one knows what Jesus was writing on the ground. The point was he did not answer them immediately. He knew the woman was caught in adultery. He knew the woman should be stoned to death. But he came with a message stronger than penalty of the law. Jesus answered them with a different aspect of the law of Moses. He told any of them that had no sin to cast the first stone. Of course, all of them knew they were sinners. They would not dare lie before God at that moment. I believe the words were anointed by the Holy Spirit and his words pierced all their hearts. All of the accusers turned, dropped their stones and walked away. Jesus was left alone with the woman. Jesus was without sin. He could have stoned her to death. He would have been exacting the law of Moses. Instead, his mercy towards her and his love for her is shown in his words to her, He did not condemn her and she should sin no more.

9 Being convicted by their conscience, those who heard it went out one by one, beginning with the eldest even to the last. Jesus was left alone, and the woman standing in the midst. 10 When Jesus had stood up and saw no one but the woman, He said to her, "Woman, where are your accusers? Did no one condemn you?"

11 She said, "No one, Lord."

Jesus said to her, "Neither do I condemn you. Go and sin no more."

The love of Jesus towards us is the same way. When we appear at the judgment seat of Christ, as all believers in Jesu will, Jesus will give us judgement or reward based on what we have done with our faith in Jesus while we lived on earth. He is the righteous judge because he triumphed over sin, death, hell and the grave. He is also the merciful compassionate savior who died for each of our sins so that if we would believe in him and confess our sins, we would be saved.

1 John 1: 9 If we confess our sins, He is faithful and just to forgive us our sins and cleanse us from all unrighteousness.

3 JOY

Joy

Joy is a fruit of the Holy Spirit. The fruit of the spirit are in each Christian because they are the characteristics of the Holy Spirit. The fruit are not always evident in all Christians because it also has to do with personal choice. For instance, I became a Christian while I was in university; I already had certain character traits, some affected by my family and heritage, some because of environment, and some because of my own choices.

Immediately after praying giving my life to Jesus, I felt as though huge weights were lifted off of me. I felt peace, joy, freedom, like I had never known. I would have been content for my salvation if that were all to it. What happened though is the more I pursued God, the more I desired His Holy presence, the more I pressed in in prayer, I found God transforming me from glory to glory. I would compare it to new levels of learning. For example, students who are in grade 3 learn certain words, math concepts, art etc. In grade 4, they build on the things they have previously learned. New things are introduced to them. There are new levels of achievement. I am a teacher and so this concept is familiar to me. There are no limits to a person's learning. Each day that I live, I endeavor to learn something new. I want to keep lifelong learning all of my life.

My life with the Holy Spirit is very similar. Each encounter of reading the Bible, praying, praising and worshipping causes me to want to know God more. The more I learn, the more I want to learn. I realize things within my own character that have changed because of my relationship with God. As a new Christian, I desired to be at church as much as possible. As we were worshipping, I gave myself wholly to God. As the minister preached, it didn't matter who it was, I felt like he was directly speaking to me. God quickened the songs to me, the prophesies, the preaching. It was like I was in heaven. I didn't know I could have the presence of God the same in my home until God revealed it to me. I had not read all the Bible before I was a Christian so I did not know scripture. One day, God quickened the following scripture to me. It jumped at me as though God were magnifying it to me.

61: 1 The Spirit of the Lord God is upon me
    because the Lord has anointed me
    to preach good news to the poor;

He has sent me to heal the broken-hearted,
    to proclaim liberty to the captives,
    and the opening of the prison to those who are bound;
2 to proclaim the acceptable year of the Lord
    and the day of vengeance of our God;
to comfort all who mourn,
3   to preserve those who mourn in Zion,
to give to them beauty
    for ashes,
the oil of joy
    for mourning,
the garment of praise
    for the spirit of heaviness,
that they might be called trees of righteousness,
    the planting of the Lord,
    that He might be glorified.

    I realized that the anointing of the LORD dwells in me because Jesus Christ dwells in me in the person of the Holy Spirit. I could stir the gifts of God with in me and God's presence would be manifest in me no matter where I was. I started singing some of the worship songs from church at home. I started praising God and worshipping. I felt the joy of God springing up me like a river from within. It is God in me that brought the joy bubbling up from within me. God revealed it to me. The Holy Spirit is our teacher; He will teach us of things to come. He will quicken the scriptures to us. His presence empowers us to live our lives more fully – enjoying each moment of it.

It is my strength

    A person with the anointing of God on him or her, is someone wholly abandoned to God, giving wholly unto God all of that person. He or she will be strong. He or she will be more than able to do all aspects of his or her life. A conqueror is someone who fight a battle or wins a competition. I was involved with all types of sports. I know what it is like to train, to practice to compete to win etc. Upon winning, I knew it was all of the practice and training that helped me to succeed. Some competitions were difficult. I had to give all of my efforts to win. I conquered.

    More than a conqueror I have also experienced. In those competitions, the team we played against or the person I played against, was not as skilled in the sport. The victory came easily. That was more than a conqueror because I won with not as much competition. I have competed at the city, and province levels. I have competed in some international competitions. There is always someone who is a conqueror. Sometimes, there is a clear win because you are more than a conqueror.

That is exactly what Jesus gave us by giving us the Holy Spirit. We have be empowered by the Holy Spirit with more than enough grace to live our lives. It requires communion with God. It requires prayer and praise and reading and studying God's word.

Romans 8: 37 No, in all these things we are more than conquerors through Him who loved us.

All believers in Jesus have the fruit of the Spirit because it is the character of the Holy Spirit. It is only by developing a strong relationship with God that we develop our fruit. Even if you try with all your might to release joy in your life, if you don't speak it by faith from your heart filled to overflowing with the Holy Spirit, it is as nothing. Whatever is not of faith is sin.

Romans 14: 23 But he who doubts is condemned if he eats, because it is not from faith, for whatever is not from faith is sin.

Salvation

There are different types of joy that a Christian can experience. The first joy you know as a Christian is the joy of salvation. It cannot be measured because it is the difference between life and death. A person has a measure of understanding of human life, but once he or she experiences the joy of salvation, the joy level jumps beyond what you could have ever known.

Colossians 1: 13 He has delivered us from the power of darkness and has transferred us into the kingdom of His dear Son, 14 in whom we have redemption through His blood, the forgiveness of sins.

I think about how it was a miracle that God reached towards me in love. I wanted to know God. I was searching for God but I was searching in Eastern Religions and the occult. I was sincere but I was never going to find God on my own. God in His mercy reached towards me and let someone share the gospel with me so I could be saved. I thank God regularly because I know it was a miracle, my salvation.

Psalm 51: 12 Restore to me the joy of Your salvation,

and uphold me with Your willing spirit.

Presence of God – brings joy

God's presence brings joy. Should you be a Christian but perhaps get angry in traffic or in events throughout your day, do like superman. Get yourself a spot alone a minute or several minutes. It can transform your life. Start thanking God for your salvation. Start thanking God for manifesting His peace in your life. Yeah, even if you don't feel it, praise God and thank Him for peace, for joy, etc. What will occur is not magic. It's not a mantra. It's God living in you empowering you to live in the joy that Jesus gave us. The joy of God's presence is your strength.

Nehemiah 8: 10 Then he said to them, "Go your way. Eat the fat, drink the sweet drink, and send portions to those for whom nothing is prepared; for this day is holy to our Lord. Do not be grieved, for the joy of the Lord is your strength."

I experienced this type of transformational change in my life driving. At one point, I had a long drive to make because I accepted a job out of town. Part of my travel involved travelling on the 401 Highway through Toronto. Ontario. Anyone who has ever driven through Toronto on that highway knows it is going to always be busy and sometimes it is stop and go. Other occasions are stop and wait. I would hate it. I didn't want to travel on that highway but it was the only way. I started carrying my Bible with me in the car. During those occasions where it was stop and wait, I would read My Bible. What happened is the drive became less important to me because I would be focused on the scripture. Sometimes, I would praise God continuously all the way home, praying in English and in tongues; singing in English and in tongues. I became so joyful the long drives energized me because I used them to build my relationship with God.

Israel army worshipping – leading in battle of Jericho

As Joshua stood ready to fight for the new land that God promised Abraham, Isaac, Jacob, Moses and all of Israel, God instructed Joshua through an angel who appeared to him. It was not a strategic plan of earth. It didn't seem logical to walk around the city and shout. Rather than questions it, Joshua obeyed God. The priests carried trumpets; the ark of the covenant, the worshippers, went before the army. They obeyed God and won the victory. The praise, the worship, the Ark of the covenant that had the Holy presence of God in it, were strategic to their victory.

Joshua 6: 2 The Lord said to Joshua, "See, I have given Jericho, its king, and mighty men of valor into your hand. 3 All the men of fighting age shall march around the city. Circle the city once. Do this for six days. 4 Seven priests shall carry seven ram's horn trumpets before the ark. On the seventh day, march around the city seven times, with the priests blowing the trumpets. 5 When they blow a long blast on the ram's horn and when you hear the trumpet sound, all the people shall shout a loud battle cry. The walls of the city will fall down, and the people will go up, every man straight ahead."

King David returned the ark to Jerusalem and there was much rejoicing because of it. He appointed priests and singers to worship and play instruments as God told Moses to appoint the Levites. Joy was released in all of Israel because the praise and worship of God brought joy to them.

1 Chronicles 15:16 Then David told the leaders of the Levites to position their brothers the singers with musical instruments, harps, lyres, and cymbals to resound with joyful songs.

If you are in a tough spot of life, start praying in tongues and worshipping God. Nothing can stand against the praise and worship of God. Your strength will be renewed and your boldness to defeat any enemy will be there.

Strength of God's people

The strength of God's people is God. His Holy presence with you quickens the joy in your spirit.

Psalm 20: 6 Now I know that the Lord saves His anointed;
   He will answer him from His holy heaven
   with the saving strength of His right hand.

Isaiah 51: 11 Therefore, the redeemed of the Lord shall return
   and come with singing to Zion,
   and everlasting joy shall be upon their head.
They shall obtain gladness and joy,
   and sorrow and mourning shall flee away.

We should be serving the LORD with gladness. There should be joy as we praise, worship, give, serve people or do our jobs. As Christians, all of the spheres of authority of our lives are expressions of our love for God or they should be. God commands us to serve Him with joy. Those who do not serve Him with joy, He corrects. If you want a religion, Christianity is not for you. It is not a part of your life like work, hobbies, sports. God is your life. He will use you in all aspects of your life. You should be joyful.

Deuteronomy 28: 47 because you did not serve the Lord your God with joy and with gladness of heart, for the abundance of all things.

Praise and worship with other believers

As Solomon prayed in dedicating the Temple that God had commanded be built, he prayed dedicating it. All of Israel rejoiced at the Temple being built and the service of dedication. There is a special joy that is released when there is praise and worship with other believers. It is a corporate anointing that comes on the people to worship and praise God. You know that those around you believe the same and you are worshipping the same God. It brings unity to the people and a corporate strength.

1 Chronicles 29:17 I know, my God, that You test the heart, and with uprightness You are pleased, so in the uprightness of my heart I have offered freely all these things, and now I have seen Your people, those present here, offer freely and joyously to You.

2 Chronicles 30:21 Then the sons of Israel present in Jerusalem kept the Feast of Unleavened Bread for seven days with great joy, and the Levites and priests praised the Lord every day, singing with loud instruments to the Lord.

At the rebuilt Temple

At the rebuilt temple, there was joy so strong there was weeping. I don't know if you have experienced this type of joy. I thank God that I have. I was not from a Christian home. My mother particularly was against my going to church. While I was pursuing Eastern religion, no one cared about it. Once I became a Christian, my family believed I had joined a cult. My mother would often try to draw me into arguments about the baptism of the Holy Spirit because she did not believe it was for the present. I would try not to argue. I tried to remain polite. I earnestly prayed for her with all my being. The day I got a phone call from a friend informing me that my mother had accepted Jesus Christ as her Saviour and had been baptized in the Holy Spirit speaking in other tongues, I kneeled in prayer thanking God. The words were like anointment. It brought such joy to my spirit, it brought joy to my soul that I thanked God weeping with joy at her salvation.

In the dedication of the rebuilt temple, some were weeping with joy. I do believe it is the same kind of joy I described. It is the joy of knowing without a doubt something for God has been accomplished. Some shouted for joy. Some wept for joy. They are not opposites; they are the same: both expressions of joy that overwhelm the human spirit.

Ezra 3:12 Now many of the older Levitical priests and chiefs of the fathers' households who had seen the first temple wept with a loud voice as the foundation of this temple was laid before their eyes, though many others shouted exuberantly for joy.

Ezra 6:16 The children of Israel, the priests and the Levites, and the rest of the descendants of the captivity kept the dedication of this house of God with joy.

Nehemiah 12:43 On that day they offered great sacrifices and rejoiced because God had given them great cause for rejoicing. The wives and the children rejoiced, too. From far away the joyful celebration of Jerusalem was heard.

If you know you do not have the fruit of joy developed as it should be, you cannot grow it yourself. You must pursue God. There are things you can do to help it to grow.

1.	Thank God for your salvation. Think of how it was a miracle that softened and transformed your life.
2.	Play praise and worship music in your home, in your car and in your mp3 player. Listen to others giving glory to God. It will compel you to start praising and worshipping. It matters what you listen to. Make it something that will release and develop the fruit of joy.
3.	Pray regularly every day. Praise. Worship. Give yourself to God fresh each day as though you are a willing vessel He can use. As you yield your whole being, body, soul and spirit, you release yourself to rely on the Holy Spirit and joy is released.
4.	Get with other believers regularly. If your church doesn't have praise and worship that excites you to worship God, go to a different church. There should be a special excitement as you worship God with other believers that is unique to the Christian church.
5.	Read your Bible prayerfully. Research the scriptures in this chapter on joy and the context of the chapters. Prayerfully confess with faith " The fruit of joy is in me because the Holy Spirit is in me."

4 PEACE

Peace

The fruit of peace is immediately imparted into a person once he or she receives Jesus Christ. The fruit may not be in full manifestation, but it is there. I love fruit – especially strawberries. I like them home grown or locally grown. Store bought are acceptable but the best is fresh. Within one strawberry there are hundreds of tiny seeds. The same is true of all-natural fruit. There are many seeds. Each seed has the potential to grow into a full plant if properly planted and cared for. As soon as you receive Christ, the fruit of peace is evident.

My salvation was rather radical as I was not going towards God but searching for Him in the wrong directions. God made a way and sent people who shared Christ with me. I had never truly known peace until I was saved. I had enjoyed life and rode it like a surf boarder rides a wave. There were ups and downs and I believed all of life was like it. Only after I received Christ did I realize that peace is God living on the inside of me. The day I was saved, I felt a heavy burden drip off me. I would describe it as if I were in iron clothing or a heavy weight; as soon as I received Christ it was off me. I felt peace. I knew I was right with God. I knew God's love for me. I knew that God would always be with me throughout my life.

The peace of God's presence is total confidence in God. The peace of God can be as an umpire. I heard Gloria Copeland say it years ago and it became my way of life. If a person is unsure of what decision to go, that both ways seem equally pleasing (of course they align with scripture) to literally pray saying God I am going to choose this way STATE IT unless you lead me differently. I submit to you Holy Spirit to let peace be my umpire.

In important decisions, God prompts me, sometimes gives me a scripture, a dream or a promise. In some decisions though, I believe in most decisions, God expects us to use wisdom and common sense. I played baseball many years and I know what power the Umpire has in a game. The final call is what the Umpire says. Not what the players say, not what the coaches say, but what the Umpire says. He makes calls about safe or out. By asking the Holy Spirit to lead me in this way, I have made serious decisions. I may not have had a clear word from God but I know the difference between his peace and approval or the lack of it.

Some Christians may not live in the full blessing of the peace of God that is available to them. For instance. There are Christians who may be caught up with the media news on a tragic event and lose their peace. They will start thinking about the horrible thing. I'm not saying we shouldn't care and pray for the families of people affected. They will watch it over and over and listen to it over and over. They will speak the negative aspects of the event to each other and fully absorb all they can concerning the negative thing. It is habit forming. They become people who talk negatively and whose point of view in life is the direct result of their fully immersing themselves in negative news.

It was many years ago but I heard Kenneth Copeland say something like "the recession – the downward economy – I will not be a part of it. He explained how he had always watched the news and discovered the negative media was affecting him spiritually. His confession impacted me and I realized that I do not have to be negative. I do not have to accept the negative news as the final news. I can trust in God's Word and God's ways and God can bless me anyway. I can let the peace of God keep me even though things are happening around me.

Psalm 91: He who dwells in the shelter of the Most High
    shall abide under the shadow of the Almighty.
2 I will say of the Lord, "He is my refuge and my fortress,
    my God in whom I trust."

Only by keeping my eyes fixed on God and His Word do I find unshakable peace. It does not mean I don't care. It does not mean I am not informed. I am a news hound. I read the news – but realize often the news given is not fully developed. There is always more than one point of view. I often compare different news sources because often certain media is biased; rarely is it without bias. I care about all people in all nations. I believe it is part of my responsibility towards the great commission. Often, I pray as a result of what I've heard or read in the media. The main difference about the old me that would get all caught up in the tragedy and the Spiritual me is that I realize God's peace in the midst of it. My heart, my inner most being is established in God's Word.

Psalm 112: 7 He shall not be afraid of evil tidings;
    his heart is fixed, trusting in the Lord.

The big difference is really how much we magnify God or perceive God. I will never believe it is God's will to bring earthquakes or tsunamis. I will never believe God wanted to kill people. My perception of God is based on God's word not the ideas of myself or any other person. God has promised hundreds of blessings to those who are in covenant with Him. God's Word clearly promises his people blessings and His comforting Holy Spirit in the midst of any situation.

Jeremiah 29: 11 For I know the plans that I have for you, says the Lord, plans for peace and not for evil, to give you a future and a hope.

The first peace I knew came from God's Holy presence. I also realize that peace can be my Umpire. I also realize that what I listen to, what I watch, what I give myself can affect my life. I choose to magnify Jesus Christ. An example of what I am speaking of can be found in the simple popular book Where is Waldo. It was very popular years ago, but there are other similar books and games for children mostly where you must search for a figure on a page that is filled with pictures or is as a scene. You search for the certain item. While searching, you see many similar items but none of them are really it. It is often hard to identify the exact figure. It can be amusing. Once you find the figure, it jumps out at you as though it were there all along. It seems magnified. Even if you turn to a different page and come back, you know where it is.

Whatever a person magnifies in his or her own life is what the person will focus on. I would like to magnify Jesus Christ. I pray it. I give myself to God so that I might see things from His points of view. Often, I admit that I do not understand why something is the way it is. Once I see things in light of eternity, I realize that it is not as important as it may seem. I also think of it differently. An example is as follows. If I were to gather some experts together a mathematical genius, a literary genius and a technological genius and I asked all three of them to write and comment on a video I showed them or to draw conclusions based on an event, all of them would have a different frame of reference. All of them would have a different perspective. To see things from God's perspective is to see things in light of eternity. God's Word is eternal.

A major concern for most governments is global warming and the environment. There are people who are well meaning but use scare tactics to make people believe the world is going to end because of pollution or global warming etc. Please understand, I believe that it is our responsibility to God to care for the earth and to do what we can to protect the environment and also all species. God's word clearly promises that the earth is going to remain until Christ returns. As long as the earth remains there are going to be seasons of planting, and harvesting.

Genesis 8: 22 While the earth remains,
seedtime and harvest,
cold and heat,
summer and winter,
and day and night
will not cease."

As Jesus was ascending into heaven, the angels spoke promising them Jesus would return for His people in the same viable way he ascended.

Acts 1: 10 While they looked intently toward heaven as He ascended, suddenly two men stood by them in white garments. 11 They said, "Men of Galilee, why stand looking toward heaven? This same Jesus, who was taken up from you to heaven, will come in like manner as you saw Him go into heaven."

The Eon or earth society as we know it will not cease until all of prophesies of Jesus are fulfilled.

Luke 21: 32 "Truly, I tell you, this generation will not pass away until all these things are fulfilled. 33 Heaven and earth will pass away, but My words will not pass away.

While my book is not specifically about the end of the world, it does need to be mentioned. There are people who are fear mongers. They magnify negative things and then scare people into believing the world will end. A Christian should never be affected by those people. Our hearts should be established in God's Word. We must read and study God's Word to understand it.

Seeing things from God's point of view or in light of eternity can only occur when a Christian is in total communion with God in total immersion with God's Spirit. It is possible to have a peace that goes beyond all things of the earth. The peace that passes understanding comes because it is not of this world – it is of the Holy Spirit or the eternal God who lives within you.

Jesus promised to send the Holy Spirit who would comfort us and keep us and teach us and live within us. To know the peace of God one must be obedient to God and be in right relationship with Him.

John 14: 15 "If you love Me, keep My commandments. 16 I will pray the Father, and He will give you another Counselor, that He may be with you forever: 17 the Spirit of truth, whom the world cannot receive, for it does not see Him, neither does it know Him. But you know Him, for He lives with you, and will be in you.

Peace that Passes Understanding

The peace that passes all understanding comes through the Holy Spirit living on the inside of us with our lives completely given to God. If peace is in an object or in money and the thing is lost, the person can lose his or her peace. If the person's peace is in relationship with eternal God, it can never be taken away. The Apostle Paul encourages the Church with his letter to the Philippians. He commands them to rejoice. He commands them to pray. He directly warns against fear or anxiety (because it is not from God). He commands us to pray and thank God believing that God will answer. Doing these things is a way to know the peace that passes all understanding.

Philippians 4: 4 Rejoice in the Lord always. Again, I will say, rejoice! 5 Let everyone come to know your gentleness. The Lord is at hand. 6 Be anxious for nothing, but in everything, by prayer and supplication with gratitude, make your requests known to God. 7 And the peace of God, which surpasses all understanding, will protect your hearts and minds through Christ Jesus.

Never believe God sent a disaster or a death or negative thing to teach people. God does not use things that would harm people to teach them. That would make God a horrible evil person. God is merciful, kind, compassionate.

When Adam and Eve sinned in Genesis 3, they caused reverberations of the results of sin in the natural world as well as with all people who ever lived. The consequence of sin is living in the curse. Adam and Eve lost their relationship with God because of their sin. Adam and Eve cursed the earth because of their sin. The earth, as beautiful as it is, is not without remnants of the curse of sin. Animals hunt and kill each other and sometimes people. There are earthquakes and Tsunamis. There are things that occur because sin exists in our world.

Genesis 3: 17 And to Adam He said, "Because you have listened to the voice of your wife and have eaten from the tree about which I commanded you, saying, 'You shall not eat of it,'

Cursed is the ground on account of you;
    in hard labor you will eat of it

all the days of your life.
18 Thorns and thistles it will bring forth for you,
    and you will eat the plants of the field.
19 By the sweat of your face
    you will eat bread
until you return to the ground,
    because out of it you were taken;
for you are dust,
    and to dust you will return."

There is hope though. Jesus Christ paid the penalty for sin by living a Holy life, dying for our sins and rising from the dead and ascending into Heaven. Jesus blood makes us holy and gives us total communion with God. By accepting Jesus, your sins are forgiven. By being baptized in the Holy Spirit, you are more than able to live your life in victory for the glory of God. It's God's covenant with you. Jesus the sinless man died so the sins of Adam could be erased or blotted out.

1 John 1: 9 If we confess our sins, He is faithful and just to forgive us our sins and cleanse us from all unrighteousness

Romans 5: 1 Therefore, since we have been justified by faith, we have peace with God through our Lord Jesus Christ, 2 through whom we also have access by faith into this grace in which we stand, and so we rejoice in hope of the glory of God.

1 Corinthians 15: 21 For since death came by man, by man came also the resurrection of the dead. 22 For as in Adam all die, even so in Christ shall all be made alive.

Your peace can be in Jesus Christ. It is possible to know peace because you live in communion with God. Rather than live in the world's system of magnifying the negative, you can live magnifying Jesus. The more you magnify Jesus, the more you live like him. His character becomes your character through the person of the Holy Spirit.

By living your life as a Christian in obedience to God's Word, the Holy Spirit will lead you and guide you all throughout your life. There are many people who do not yet know Jesus or have the confidence of relationship with Him. By praying, rejoicing, thanking God and doing all we can to improve the lives of those around us, we can affect our world. We can shine as lights pointing the way to Jesus. We are in the world but we do not live by the world's systems or even by our senses only. God's word is established. God's Word is eternal. Faith in God will always result in peace.

Psalm 143: 10 Teach me to do Your will,
    for You are my God;
may Your good spirit
    lead me onto level ground.

As part of having God's word in our hearts, it brings peace; we delight to do God's will.

Psalm 40: 8 I delight to do Your will, O my God;
    Your law is within my inward parts."

Peacemakers

Matthew 5: 9 Blessed are the peacemakers,
    for they shall be called the sons of God.

It is possible for a Christian to take authority in the realms of the earth and be a peace maker. There may be a gathering of people complaining or grumbling about something. Usually people that complain daily are complaining about family or bosses or work etc. I mean here in North America. In other countries where Christians are literally running and hiding for their lives, they don't complain much.

In our society, it is possible to achieve some financial wealth and then complain it is not enough. It could be true that you are paid as well as you could be or that you should be paid more. Focusing on what you do have instead of what you don't have is the answer. Giving thanks to God for your job, your family etc. Pray and ask God how you can be a more excellent employee or a more excellent family role model. If we fix our eyes on Jesus, instead of what we don't have, God will bless us and of course we will be much happier.

Years ago, I remember a professor teaching us with half a glass of water. He asked us if it was partly empty or partly full. Some people expressed their opinions. I am saying that every Christian can choose each day to focus on the positive aspects. It is a decision that affects your life daily.

Priestly blessing

After receiving the commandments and other Levitical laws of God, Moses was given a prayer for the priests to say over the people to bless them. Truly this is a prayer directly commanded by God Himself. It contains aspects that cover the areas of man's life. It expresses God's sincere loving desire to care for us.

God's blessing means SHALOM peace – nothing missing and nothing broken. It means total prosperity of spirit, soul and body. That is the type of peace God has for those in covenant with Him. God's face shining on you is His favour. God wants you to have favour with all kinds of people. It is a special something that God places over you so that you always get the best He has for you. God's countenance upon us means He is listening to our prayers. He is watching and caring for you as a parent would care for his or her children. Please accept the kind of peace I am talking about. It isn't for only some. It is for all who believe in Jesus Christ.

Numbers 6: 22 The Lord spoke to Moses, saying: 23 Speak to Aaron and to his sons, saying, This is how you will bless the children of Israel, saying to them,

24 The Lord bless you
   and keep you;
25 the Lord make His face to shine upon you,
   and be gracious unto you;
26 the Lord lift His countenance upon you,
   and give you peace.

Avoid strife

Strife or complaining, grumbling, negative talk, abrupt conversations with people and fighting among people is the opposite or peace.

Be the thermostat not the thermometer

I am not the originator of this saying but I can't remember where I got it from or I would credit them. A thermometer is used to take the temperature of a person. The thermostat is used to change the temperature. Similarly, Christians are called to be thermostats. By our good conversation and our kinds deeds and lives we can influence those around us. The people who want to be grumpy will hate us. The devil will hate us, because we keep magnifying the positive. We keep thanking God for what He has given us.

We do unto others as we would have them do to us. We love and show respect for all humans and animals. We should be like living epistles – living witnesses of God's mercy towards people.

Abraham

Abraham shows this type of peace and snuffs out any strife between his nephew and himself. The blessing of God was on Abraham. Prosperity was Abraham's because promised to bless him in all areas of life. Lot was only wealthy because he was with Abraham. A day came when the servants of Abraham and the servants of Lot were fighting over their herds. They were family. There was covetousness in Lot. He wanted to be wealthy even if it meant strife. He would get the most no matter what it meant to the family. Abraham was not like that at all. Abraham realized peace was more important than any amount of wealth. He had special wisdom from God. He gave Lot the choice of land. God had given all the land to Abraham – not Lot. Abraham in his generosity let LOT choose which way he wanted to go. Lot being covetous, chose the best for himself not thinking or caring about his uncle or their family.

Genesis 13: So Abram said to Lot, "Let there be no strife, I ask you, between me and you, and between my herdsmen and your herdsmen, for we are close relatives. 9 Is not the whole land before you? Please separate from me. If you will go to the left, then I will go to the right, or if you take the right, then I will go to the left."

Because of this decision, God prospered Abraham even more. You cannot love things or money more than peace or more than people.

James

In the new testament, after the Apostle Paul received Christ, he preached Jesus Christ to the Jews but he was not well received and beaten, thrown in jail etc. Paul went to Europe and preached Jesus to the non-Jews or Gentiles. They were worshippers of other gods and did not know the things of covenant relationship with God. The Apostle Paul preached Jesus the Messiah. Paul had been a Pharisee so he knew all the Messianic prophecies that Jesus had fulfilled. He also had encountered Jesus personally and his life was transformed by it. Paul preached and the Church began to be multiplied among the Gentiles.

There was strife between the disciples and followers of Jesus who knew Jesus personally and the teachings of the Apostle Paul. The Jewish believers believed all of the people had to become Jews first and keep all the Jewish laws and also accept Christ. The Apostle Paul didn't teach it. Paul believed they only need receive Jesus Christ to be saved. The Apostle James rose up and was given wisdom by God. He brought peace and a solution that brought peace both to the Jewish believers and the Apostle Paul.

Acts 15: 13 After they had become silent, James answered, "Brothers, listen to me. 14 Simon has declared how God first visited the Gentiles to take from among them a people for His name. 15 With this the words of the prophets agree. As it is written:

16 'After this I will return,
    and I will rebuild the tabernacle of David, which has fallen;
I will rebuild its ruins,
    and I will set it up;[a]
17 that the rest of men may seek the Lord,
    and all the Gentiles who are called by My name,[b]
says the Lord who does all these things.'[c]
18   Known to God are all His works since the beginning of the world.

19 "Therefore my judgment is that we should not trouble those of the Gentiles who are turning to God, 20 but that we write to them to abstain from food offered to idols, from sexual immorality, from strangled animals, and from blood. 21 For Moses has had in every city since early generations those who preach him, being read in the synagogues every Sabbath."

God's wisdom though James meant there was no division in that early church. It meant peace.

The words that we speak

The words that we speak can bring life or death, cursing or blessing. The words we speak can totally quench and squash strife. I have witnessed it myself and God has given me special wisdom so He has inspired me to speak peace into a strife situation in the following way. Even if the person is yelling in anger, treat the person with respect and kindness and love as though that is the way the person was treating you. It takes all the wind out of them. They lose their argument because they have no one to fight with.

Proverbs 15: 1

A soft answer turns away wrath,

but grievous words stir up anger.

2 The tongue of the wise uses knowledge aright,
  but the mouth of fools pours out foolishness.

Jesus promised to give us the peace that was beyond all the earthly realms.

John 14: 27 Peace I leave with you. My peace I give to you. Not as the world gives do I give to you. Let not your heart be troubled, neither let it be afraid.

The disciples were gathered in the upper room. Jesus appeared in their midst – not going through the door. They were frightened. His first words were " Peace be with you." He spoke peace.

They realized it was Jesus and not an apparition. They could see the wounds in his hands and feet and the hole in his side. Jesus gathered them unto Himself and said "Peace be with you" once more. He commissioned them to preach the good news of salvation. He breathed on them and told them to receive the Holy Spirit. This was before Pentecost. The resurrected Jesus brought peace by giving the Holy Spirit to the disciples before they had the experience of the Baptism in the Holy Spirit.

John 20: 19 On the evening of that first day of the week, the doors being locked where the disciples were assembled, for fear of the Jews, Jesus came and stood in their midst, and said to them, "Peace be with you." 20 When He had said this, He showed them His hands and His side. The disciples were then glad when they saw the Lord.

21 So Jesus said to them again, "Peace be with you. As My Father has sent Me, even so I send you." 22 When He had said this, He breathed on them and said to them, "Receive the Holy Spirit. 23 If you forgive the sins of anyone, they are forgiven them. If you retain the sins of anyone, they are retained."

Peace in God's Word is the only true peace. Peace in things or in people can change but God's Word is established. If you know Jesus but do not know the type of peace I have discussed, you can know it.

1.   Should you have any sin in your life, confess it to God and accept Jesus' blood as forgiveness and know that you are right with God.
2.   Examine your life to see what you are doing with the majority of your day. I mean besides work such as watching 2-3 hours of TV or hanging out

at friends etc. Find a way to give yourself 1 hour a day to read the Bible and pray. Give yourself to God's Word. Get any version of the Bible you can understand. Pray for yourself, your family, your region. Pray to know God more. Literally pray the scriptures over yourself.

Example pray " I have the peace that passes all understanding because Jesus gave it to me." Literally accept God's word for yourself as though it were personally written to you.

3.   Watch your words. It's impossible to do without the help of the Holy Spirit. Literally pray: Holy Spirit set a guard over my mouth. Help to know if I say something that is not pleasing to you. Help me to live pleasing in my words." God will correct you. You can expect it.   In major Spiritual revivals, the language the people were speaking changed because it all became more positive and encouraging.

4.   Pray that God will use you to speak peace into people's lives shining the light of Christ in your spheres of influence.

5.   Thank God for each thing He has done for you such as salvation, healing, deliverance. Speak your testimony of answered prayers to others so they will be encouraged and their faith can be encouraged.

5 PATIENCE, FORBEARANCE

Patience, Forbearance

The fruit of patience and forbearance aren't simply waiting and remaining calm. Patience is waiting in faith believing God and holding on to God's Word until the miracle or thing we are praying for manifests in the physical realm. The waiting doing the right thing repeatedly is the forbearance part.

The unsaved soul does not demonstrate patience.

1.   The soul and patience – the unsaved soul (mind, will emotions) of a person is selfish and ego driven. The soul hates waiting. The selfish soul believes the world owes him or her. Often what will manifest is abrupt complaining, and grumbling which could lead to further sins.
2.   The spiritual man being renewed by the Holy Spirit is kind, patient waiting, believing for the best, remaining positive, and constantly seeking opportunities to help others.

God is so merciful towards us that it may seem He is a push over or someone easy to take advantage of. In fact, He is patient, waiting for people to repent. Sometimes, while God is giving chance after chance for a person to repent, it seems God is doing nothing. He is not doing nothing; He is being patient. The following passage explains God's mercy towards people. Some of those people are wicked and if humans were to judge them, we would eliminate them or remove them from authority. God gives chances to every person on earth to receive Jesus as Saviour and Lord. God sometimes with his patience withholds judgement.

Some people I have witnessed to about Jesus Christ have asked questions such as why does God allow these horrible things to occur on earth. The truth is that God is waiting, giving the person mercy so that he or she may repent and be saved. Usually if there is someone doing evil, others are involved. God is merciful in His waiting. If He were to judge them immediately those people would be sentenced to hell eternally. What seems to some as God not caring is really God' mercy even towards the wicked and people around them. It is tough for us as humans to understand because we would of course instantly judge a wicked person and condemn him or her.

I can tell you that I thank God for His extra mercy shown to me. If He had judged me by any of my sins, I would have no chance of salvation. God showed me mercy and showed me mercy and continued to show me mercy until finally one day by His mercy and grace He softened my heart and drew me to Himself so I could be saved. It transformed my life completely.

I give no excuse for wicked people in authority. I am not condoning sin and wickedness; I am explaining why there isn't instant judgement on wicked rulers or corrupt people with positions of authority.

What if God

Romans 9: 22 What if God, willing to show His wrath and to make His power known, endured with much patience the vessels of wrath prepared for destruction, 23 in order to make known the riches of His glory on the vessels of mercy, which He previously prepared for glory, 24 even us, whom He has called, not from the Jews only, but also from the Gentiles? 25 As indeed He says in Hosea:

God explains that He will draw people to Himself that were not His people. God will draw them to Himself. God gives chances to each person to receive Him. I don't know the number of chances; I believe each prayer we pray for a person, releases Angels and people to draw our loved ones to God. It is like gravity. God's love is like a magnet that pulls people towards Him. They don't have to accept it. It is pure, holy, kind, compassionate, enlightening, loving, giving etc. People can be drawn or they can fight against it and escape it. God gives people many chances to repent and turn to Him.

"I will call those who were not My people, 'My people,'
    and her who was not beloved, 'Beloved,' "[g]
26 and,
"In the place where it was said to them,
    'You are not My people,'
there they shall be called 'sons of the living God.' "[h]
27 Isaiah also cries out concerning Israel:
"Though the number of the children of Israel be like the sand of the sea,
    a remnant shall be saved.[i]
28 For He will finish the work, and cut it short in righteousness,
    because the Lord will make a quick work upon the earth."[j]

Long patient waiting for the fruit of the earth

The fruit of patience is commanded. The scripture discusses the seasons of agriculture and how the farmer must wait for the proper season to bring its harvest. There is a process of the crops forming and becoming ripe. We are as fruit in the kingdom of God. There is an admonition not to grumble or complain) like a fleshly carnal person) but to keep focused on Jesus.

The apostle also tells us to remember the prophets who would get a word from God and sometimes, often, they were not listened to or they were mocked or scorned or even murdered because of their words. The example of Job is a strong image because Job, a righteous man endured horrible things in his life but remained faithful to God and kept his faith in God as being good. Finally, at the end of the book of Job, God spoke blessings audibly over him and condemned his wicked friends who were accusing him of being a sinner. Job was righteous. He was not a sinner. He was blessed by God in his later years with twice as much as he had in his earlier years. God prospered and rewarded Job but it wasn`t instant.

James 5: 7 Therefore be patient, brothers, until the coming of the Lord. Notice how the farmer waits for the precious fruit of the earth and is patient with it until he receives the early and late rain. 8 You also be patient. Establish your hearts, for the coming of the Lord is drawing near. 9 Do not grumble against one another, brothers, lest you be condemned. Look, the Judge is standing at the door.

10 My brothers, take the prophets, who spoke in the name of the Lord, as an example of suffering and patience. 11 Indeed we count them happy who endure. You have heard of the patience of Job and have seen the purpose of the Lord, that the Lord is very gracious and merciful.

Faith and patience inherit the promises

Faith is the substance of things hoped for. (Hebrews 11:1) Faith is a spiritual force; it is an elemental force in Christian life. Without faith, you cannot please God. Faith is necessary but also is patience. Together faith or believing God and patience, doing all you can do and being consistent and praying and confessing God`s word and continuing to do it over and over and over until you can see the manifestation of the miracle is required to inherit the promises of God.

Hebrews 6: 9 But though we speak in this manner, we are persuaded of better things for you, things that accompany salvation, 10 for God is not unjust so as to forget your work and labor of love that you have shown for His name, in that you have ministered to the saints and continue ministering. 11 We desire that every one of you show the same diligence for the full assurance of hope to the end, 12 so that you may not be lazy, but imitators of those who through faith and patience inherit the promises.

An excellent example of this scripture is Abram and Sara. They received the promises of God concerning having an heir that would be numerous and inherit the land that was promised. It was almost 30 years before the miracle occurred. Through it they were transformed. Abram became Abraham and Sara became Sarah. They received the answers to their prayers but it was almost 30 years before it occurred.

Romans 4: 16 Therefore the promise comes through faith, so that it might be by grace, that the promise would be certain to all the descendants, not only to those who are of the law, but also to those who are of the faith of Abraham, who is the father of us all 17 (as it is written, "I have made you a father of many nations"[c]) before God whom he believed, and who raises the dead, and calls those things that do not exist as though they did.

19 And not being weak in faith, he did not consider his own body to be dead (when he was about a hundred years old), nor yet the deadness of Sarah's womb. 20 He did not waver at the promise of God through unbelief, but was strong in faith, giving glory to God, 21 and being fully persuaded that what God had promised, He was able to perform. 22 Therefore "it was credited to him as righteousness.

Of sowing and reaping

Seasons of the earth – planting, watering, harvesting

Mark 4: "Listen! And take note: A sower went out to sow. 4 As he sowed, some seed fell beside the path, and the birds of the air came and devoured it. 5 Some seed fell on rocky ground, where it did not have much soil, and soon it sprang up because it did not have deep soil. 6 But when the sun rose, it was scorched. And because it had no root, it withered away. 7 Other seed fell among thorns, and the thorns grew up and choked it, and it yielded no grain. 8 And other seed fell on good ground, and it yielded grain that sprang up and increased by thirty, sixty, or a hundred times as much."

9 Then He said to them, "He who has ears to hear, let him hear."

Meaning of the parable

Jesus taught the people using parables or stories that explained deep spiritual things in ordinary human terms. He spoke of the seed that was sown into different types of soil and told what happened in each type of soil. The people he was speaking to were farmers so they understood that seed sown onto rocky ground could not bare because the roots could not sustain the plant because the rock prevented it. The seed sown onto a path or walkway would be tread upon and have no chance for growth. The seeds sown in thorny ground would be choked out by the weeds and thorns. Finally, the seed sown on good ground would produce fruit: 30, 60, 100-fold.

Truly the scripture applies to the word of God being sown into people`s lives and the condition of the human heart or soul determines the results of the seed sown. It is not instant. There is a process of growth. There is a measuring of growth.

Mark 4: The Parable of the Sower Explained

13 Then He said to them, "Do you not understand this parable? How then will you understand all the parables? 14 The sower sows the word. 15 These are those beside the path, where the word is sown. But when they hear, Satan comes immediately and takes away the word which is sown in their hearts. 16 Others, likewise, are seed sown on rocky ground, who, when they hear the word, immediately receive it with gladness, 17 but have no root in themselves, and so endure for a time. Afterward, when affliction or persecution rises for the word's sake, immediately they fall away. 18 And others are seed sown among thorns, the ones who hear the word. 19 But the cares of this world, and the deceitfulness of riches, and the desires for other things entering in choke the word, and it proves unfruitful. 20 Still others are seed sown on good ground, those who hear the word, and receive it, and bear fruit: thirty, sixty, or a hundred times as much."

The Parable of the Growing Seed

Once more Jesus uses a parable to teach the people about the growth process of planting seed. First the seed is placed n the ground; next the seed sprouts like a leaf. The blade is formed; the head is formed, the full seed in the head. The corn starts with one seed but during its growing period develops and becomes a full ripe corn plant with more than one cob of corn on it. It seems so simple, but it is a teaching tool to show us, there is a process to life on earth; there is a process to spiritual growth also.

Mark 4: 26 He said, "The kingdom of God is like a man who scatters seed on the ground. 27 He sleeps and rises night and day, and the seed sprouts and grows; he does not know how. 28 For the earth bears fruit by itself: first the blade, then the head, then the full seed in the head. 29 But when the grain is ripe, immediately he applies the sickle because the harvest has come."

Seed as a mustard seed – mighty tree

Once more Jesus uses a parable of growth of a mustard seed. It is a tiny seed in comparison to most seeds. Once that tony seed springs up, it can grow larger than shrubs or trees and it can become a shelter to people and birds. Faith, even if it is as small as a mustard seed can produce a mighty miracle. There is a process of sowing and reaping.

Mark 4: 30 He said, "To what shall we liken the kingdom of God, or with what parable shall we compare it? 31 It is like a grain of mustard seed which, when it is sown in the ground, is the smallest seed on earth. 32 Yet when it is sown, it grows up and becomes greater than all shrubs, and shoots out great branches, so that the birds of the air may nest in its shade."

Seed as a seed to move mountains

In this parable of the seed Jesus talks about the power of the seed. Even faith the size of a mustard seed can move a mountain. What seems impossible to humans, is possible to God. It is faith and patience that determines the results. In the particular instance where the disciples could not heal the boy, although they tried was because Jesus said there were different kinds of healing. This kind only could come through a lifestyle of prayer and fasting. It was a fasting and prayer lifestyle – process – dedication to God that brought about the deliverance of that boy.

Matthew 17: 20 Jesus said to them, "Because of your unbelief. For truly I say to you, if you have faith as a grain of mustard seed, you will say to this mountain, 'Move from here to there,' and it will move. And nothing will be impossible for you. 21 But this kind does not go out except by prayer and fasting."

Continual knocking

Jesus talks about enduring prayer or repeated prayer or prayer that occurs over a duration as being effective. Some prayers, a person prays once; other prayers are a constant faith and patience type of prayer, confession, thanking God before the miracle occurs. The example is the man who keeps knocking until the door is open and he receives his bread.

Luke 11: 5 Then He said to them, "Which of you has a friend and shall go to him at midnight and say to him, 'Friend, lend me three loaves, 6 for a friend of mine on his journey has come to me, and I have nothing to set before him'; 7 and he will answer from within, 'Do not trouble me; the door is now shut, and my children are with me in bed; I cannot rise and give you anything'? 8 I say to you, though he will not rise and give him anything because he is his friend, yet because of his persistence he will rise and give him as much as he needs.

In the same way Jesus tells us to knock and seek and keep on seeking and finally to ask and keep on asking, keep on knocking – to pray and keep on praying if we want results with God. It is not instant. There is a pattern of repetition and duration for the miracle to manifest.

Luke 119 "And I tell you, ask, and it will be given to you; seek, and you will find; knock, and it will be opened to you. 10 For everyone who asks receives, and he who seeks finds, and to him who knocks it will be opened.

The unjust judge

The parable of the widow pleading with the unjust judge is encouraging because it does not depend on the righteousness of the person in authority but rather the perseverance of the widow. She demanded justice to be given to her. Even though he was corrupt, she kept coming constantly in front of him demanding justice. He did not give her the request because he was good or kind or any reason other than the matter of her coming was constant and he wanted to get rid of her. The fact was, he gave her the request.

If even an unjust person will grant justice, God most certainly will avenge His people who are constantly praying. God most certainly avenge them. The key point is faith that God will execute just judgement. There may be faith and patience required in the duration until the manifestation.

Luke 18: The Parable of the Widow and the Judge

18 He told them a parable to illustrate that it is necessary always to pray and not lose heart. 2 He said: "In a city there was a judge who did not fear God or regard man. 3 And a widow was in that city. She came to him, saying, 'Avenge me against my adversary.'

4 "He would not for a while. Yet afterward he said to himself, 'Though I do not fear God or respect man, 5 yet because this widow troubles me, I will avenge her, lest by her continual coming she will weary me.'"

6 And the Lord said, "Hear what the unjust judge says. 7 And shall not God avenge His own elect and be patient with them, who cry day and night to Him? 8 I tell you, He will avenge them speedily. Nevertheless, when the Son of Man comes, will He find faith on the earth?"

A tear with God is as a thousand to us

God's perspective is different than ours because He is eternal: He sees the past, the present and the future. Should God say soon – it may be more than a thousand years by our measurement as humans. The faith is in God being just and righteous – not in the duration of judgement being executed.

2 Peter 3: 8 But, beloved, do not be ignorant of this one thing, that with the Lord one day is as a thousand years, and a thousand years as one day. 9 The Lord is not slow concerning His promise, as some count slowness. But He is patient with us, because He does not want any to perish, but all to come to repentance.

God's perspective

God sees things eternally and He knows all things also. His ways are beyond what a human can conceive of. In comparison, an ant has some type of brain. It does certain things and cares for itself and its family. The ant cannot conceive of the things a human being can. The ant doesn't comprehend why we don't want it on our picnic table or our drink rim. In the same measure, a human has no concept of why God does something or doesn't do something.

I give my own example here. I would have never conceived of myself being so happy, enjoying God's blessing on my life and my relationship with Him the day I accepted Christ. I had no idea how awesome God would show His love towards me. God's mercy towards me has been constant and He has transformed me from glory to glory into His image. I am praying that I will continue to be transformed all of my life on the earth as well as in the afterlife. There is so much of God to learn about. There are so many amazing things in the earth; the new heavens and new earth will be even more awesome. To be in the constant presence of God, creator of all things, will be joy beyond all earthly measure.

God sees things from an eternal point of view – Gods ways not our ways – limits of human

Isaiah 55: 8 For My thoughts are not your thoughts,
   nor are your ways My ways,
   says the Lord.
9 For as the heavens are higher than the earth,
   so are My ways higher than your ways,
   and My thoughts than your thoughts.

Covenant God Mercy

God's divine love towards us can be seen in his continual making of covenants with people throughout the thousands of years in scripture. Not only does he make the covenants, but He has faithfully kept them. The words He promised thousands of years ago to Noah, He still keeps. The promises of God to Abraham have all come to pass. The promises of God to Moses are true today. God keeps His word over thousands of years; His promises are sure. All of the covenants showed His love towards us and finally the ultimate covenant of the LORD Jesus Christ giving his life to redeem us ushering in a new covenant of faith.

Psalm 105: 8 He remembers His covenant forever,
   the word that He commanded, to a thousand generations,
9 that covenant He made with Abraham,
   and His oath to Isaac,
10 and confirmed to Jacob as a decree,
   and to Israel for an everlasting covenant,
11 saying, "To you I will give the land of Canaan

God waited for a godly seed to come out of Adam – Noah was first
God waited for a godly people on earth Abraham, Moses.
God waited for Israel – knew the sins and lead her though wilderness 40 years
God`s mercy towards Israel that in any judgement, always a hope of revival because of His blood covenant with Israel.

The Covenant made with Moses about keeping the commandments is true today. God's Word is His will expressed to us. If we will keep the Word of God constantly in our hearts and lives, we will align with His word. Jesus Christ fulfilled all of the laws of Moses and all of the requirements of all of the covenants so faith in Jesus Christ releases all the covenant blessing towards us who believe in Jesus Christ. Not only is the Word of God what we live by, but God Himself writes the Word of God into our hearts and it becomes a part of our lives – we become one with God's Word.

Deuteronomy 8: 1 You must carefully keep all the commandments that I am commanding you today, so that you may live, and multiply, and go in and possess the land which the Lord swore to your fathers. 2 You must remember that the Lord your God led you all the way these forty years in the wilderness, to humble you, and to prove you, to know what was in your heart, whether you would keep His commandments or not. 3 He humbled you and let you suffer hunger, and fed you with manna, which you did not know, nor did your fathers know, that He might make you know that man does not live by bread alone; but man lives by every word that proceeds out of the mouth of the Lord. 4 Your clothing did not wear out on you, nor did your feet swell these forty years. 5 You must also consider in your heart that, as a man disciplines his son, so the Lord your God disciplines you.

God's mercy towards us even if we sin, he forgives us

Psalm 103: 7 He made known His ways to Moses,
  His acts to the people of Israel.
8 The Lord is merciful and gracious,
  slow to anger, and abounding in mercy.

God is patient with us – He knows us in all our frailties but also sees us as we will be transformed by his glory. In the presence of God, we are transformed into His image and likeness. It is a continuous coming to God and yielding of ourselves that produces Godly character in us.

2 Corinthians 3: 17 Now the Lord is the Spirit. And where the Spirit of the Lord is, there is liberty. 18 But we all, seeing the glory of the Lord with unveiled faces, as in a mirror, are being transformed into the same image from glory to glory by the Spirit of the Lord.

Although we are filled with the Spirit and living on the earth – our body will be transformed into an eternal one. We will live throughout eternity with God, learning about Him and being transformed from glory to glory.

1 Corinthians 15: 20 But now is Christ risen from the dead and become the first fruits of those who have fallen asleep. 21 For since death came by man, by man came also the resurrection of the dead. 22 For as in Adam all die, even so in Christ shall all be made alive. 23 But every man in his own order: Christ the first fruits; afterward, those who are Christ's at His coming. 24 Then comes the end when He will deliver up the kingdom to God the Father, when He puts an end to all rule and all authority and power. 25 For He will reign until He has put all enemies under His feet. 26 The last enemy that will be destroyed is death. 27 For He "has put all things under His feet."[a] But when He says, "all things are put under Him," it is revealed that He, who has put all things under Him, is the exception. 28 When all things are subjected to Him, then the Son Himself will also be subject to Him who put all things under Him, that God may be all in all.

6 GENTLENESS, MEEKNESS

Gentleness, Meekness

The fruit of gentleness is showing kindness or mercy in one's character. It is evident in demeanor or personality, attitude and in deeds. It is often associated as a parent with a child. The parent may teach the child gently and with true love. It could be as a tender, gentle, kind, soft word or touch or teaching. It resembles the Character of the Holy Spirit. Often the Holy Spirit is depicted as a dove because of the appearance like a dove over him at his water baptism by John. Also, Jesus sent the Holy Spirit to comfort us after he ascended into heaven. Doves are very gentle and they will be scared away by any abrupt motion or word. The Holy Spirit is grieved by sin, and injustice. Part of the gentle character is truth, purity. Often instruction or teaching is taking place when one shows gentleness towards another.

Meekness is the opposite of pride. It is similar to gentleness. It is humility.

John 14: 17 the Spirit of truth, whom the world cannot receive, for it does not see Him, neither does it know Him. But you know Him, for He lives with you, and will be in you.

John 14: 26 But the Counselor, the Holy Spirit, whom the Father will send in My name, will teach you everything and remind you of all that I told you. 27 Peace I leave with you. My peace I give to you. Not as the world gives do I give to you. Let not your heart be troubled, neither let it be afraid.

God with Jonah – plant – teaching of Jonah

Jonah the prophet who finally delivered the message to the people of Nineveh knew that God was forgiving. He had warned the people that if they did not repent, God was going to pour out judgement on them, so they repented. All the people repented including the king. They fasted and prayed. God had mercy on them and spared them. Jonah got angry about it. God compelled him to deliver the message and then God softened their hearts and the people repented. Jonah grumbled about it feeling as though he wasted his efforts in going and giving the message. Jonah's character is lacking in mercy or genteelness completely. Jonah goes and sulks on a rock and it is hot and Jonah is angry at God for forgiving the people. It was true the people were exceedingly wicked; it was also true; they repented. Jonah did not understand God's mercy. In spite of his character flaws, God causes a plant to grow near Jonah to shade him and cover him.

Jonah was moved by his physical comfort. He was glad about the plant. God used the plant to teach Jonah about mercy and gentleness in a kind and loving way. The plant withered and died and Jonah was hot and angry. He was mad at God; he wished he would die. God uses the plant as an illustration to teach Jonah. Jonah was angry the plant died; God used it as a chance to show how Jonah cared for one plant; God certainly cared for the life of each person in Nineveh and all the animals. God could have been angry at Jonah for his attitude, but God showed mercy on him and used a subtle example to teach a profound truth that God is merciful towards all people – even the most sinful. If a person will repent or turn to God, God will show compassion on him or her.

Jonah 4: 6 Then the Lord God appointed a plant, and it grew up over Jonah to provide shade over his head, to provide comfort from his grief. And Jonah was very happy about the plant. 7 But at dawn the next day, God appointed a worm to attack the plant so that it withered. 8 When the sun rose, God appointed a scorching east wind, and the sun beat upon the head of Jonah so that he became faint and asked that he might die. He said, "It is better for me to die than to live."

9 Then God said to Jonah, "Is it right for you to be angry about the plant?"

And Jonah replied, "It is right for me to be angry, even to death."

10 The Lord said, "You are troubled about the plant for which you did not labor and did not grow. It came up in a night and perished in a night. 11 Should I not, therefore, be concerned about Nineveh, that great city, in which there are more than a hundred and twenty thousand people, who do not know their right hand from their left, and also many animals?"

Hosea

The prophet Hosea was instructed by God to go marry a harlot. He did. She cheated on him with other lovers and was unfaithful. She ended up a slave with nothing, not even clothing. God instructed her to go once more and redeem her. Hosea found the woman and purchased her for himself. He spoke kindly towards her. He loves her although she had not been faithful. He lets her live with him and treats her with compassion. It is because he is acting out the scene of Israel's unfaithfulness to God. Israel was worshipping other gods. Israel was not showing love towards God. But God's covenant with Israel compelled Him by love to care for her even though all her choices were wrong. His gentleness towards her and his willingness to declare a prostitute as his wife shows his meekness.

1 Then the Lord said to me, "Go, again, love a woman who is loved by a lover and is committing adultery, just as the Lord loves the children of Israel, who look to other gods and love raisin cakes."

2 So I purchased her for myself for fifteen shekels of silver, and for a homer of barley, and a half homer of barley. 3 Then I said to her, "You will remain with me many days. You will not play the whore, and you will not belong to another man. And also I will be with you."

4 For the children of Israel will remain many days without a king and without a prince, without a sacrifice and without a standing stone, and without an ephod and teraphim. 5 Afterward the children of Israel will return and seek the Lord their God and David their king. They will come in fear to the Lord and to His goodness in the latter days.

God's mercy shown through Hosea towards his harlot wife same gentleness God shows towards Israel. God loved Israel so much that although Israel broke covenant with God, God kept covenant with Israel. God waited for Israel to repent and return to God. Eventually, God Himself purchased us by the blood of Jesus shed for us.

I have witnessed this spirit of gentleness in my own mother, not only towards me but towards many. There are so many instances, I could write a long chapter on it alone. I remember the incident clearly. We lived in the inner city where it once had been a nice ethnic neighborhood that was safe. After they put a Casino downtown, the people who parked on our streets were different.

There were often prostitutes who would frequent our neighborhood. One day after supper, early evening, we heard a noise; a car screeched. Thump outside in our yard. We didn't know what it was. There was a body of a young woman on our lawn. She had been severely abused and beaten, bloody. She was breathing but not able to speak or move. Some of the neighbours started to gather to see about the newest event in our neigbourhood.

My mother got water and a cloth and washed her face and prayed for her and patted her and spoke softly to her as though she were her daughter. One of the men put his coat over her to cover her nakedness. An ambulance came and the people warned us about the blood because she was a regular and she had aids.

The gentleness my mother showed towards that woman was God's love. I saw it. She did not judge the woman; she cared for her and loved her.

Jesus with the children

Jesus showed a gentle spirit towards the children. Rather than consider them as unimportant, he encouraged that they be brought to him and he blessed them. He cared enough for them, he imparted a spiritual blessing.

Matthew 19: 14 But Jesus said, "Let the little children come to Me, and do not forbid them. For to such belongs the kingdom of heaven." 15 He laid His hands on them and departed from there.

Jesus praying over Jerusalem

Jesus was on a mountain observing Jerusalem and he knew he would be betrayed. He knew that people would turn against him. He knew that the people would be unfaithful to God. He also saw how much God loved Jerusalem. He wept over it as a person would weep over a child or an unfaithful spouse. His words reflect his genteelness towards Israel. He gives the image of a hen gathering her chicks. Once more a parent with child image is used. God expressed a parental kind of desire to comfort and protect Israel.

Matthew 23: 37 "O Jerusalem, Jerusalem, you who kill the prophets and stone those who are sent to you, how often I would have gathered your children together as a hen gathers her chicks under her wings, but you would not! 38 Look, your house is left to you desolate. 39 For I tell you, you shall not see Me again until you say, 'Blessed is He who comes in the name of the Lord.'[a]"

Luke 19: 41 When He came near, He beheld the city and wept over it, 42 saying, "If you, even you, had known even today what things would bring you peace! But now they are hidden from your eyes.

Without guile – as Nathaniel

A person without guile is someone who is gentle, kind, merciful, forgiving. Jesus spotted Nathaniel and prophetically spoke a word of wisdom about him. Nathaniel realized it revealed his inner character and wanted to know how Jesus knew him. Jesus explains that he knew him as soon as he saw him earlier by a fig tree. Jesus could prophetically see and discern people by the Holy Spirit. He does not give this same compliment to any other person.

John 1: 47 Jesus saw Nathanael coming to Him and said concerning him, "Here is an Israelite indeed, in whom is no guile."

48 Nathanael said to Him, "How do You know me?"

Jesus answered him, "Before Philip called you, when you were under the fig tree, I saw you."

The Apostle Paul

The Apostle Paul uses kind tender words about those he had led to Jesus Christ. He speaks of them as they were his own children. Often a wet nurse was someone hired to feed the child until it could feed himself. The apostle Paul says they are cherished and he would even give his life for them. It is the love that is innocent, kind, gentle, nurturing.

1 Thessalonians 2: 7 But we were gentle among you, like a nurse caring for her own children. 8 So having great love toward you, we were willing to impart to you not only the gospel of God but also our own lives, because you were dear to us.

Kind

Lepers were not only people who experienced pain and loss of fingers and toes and limbs etc. by the disease, they also were outcasts. They could not be with their families; they were not permitted to be in gatherings or in public places. They were to live outside the city. Leprosy is highly contagious. If a leper were to enter a city, he or she could be stoned to death. Jesus touching the leper and healing him – possibly not touched by any other person – fear of unclear etc. Most people did not go anywhere near a leper. They did not receive hugs or kisses from family or friends. They did not receive comforting touch unless it was from each other. They were isolated into leper colonies.

A leper risked his life to go to Jesus in public. He spoke that if Jesus would will it, Jesus could heal him. Jesus spoke the word the man wanted to hear – it was his will the man be healed. Also, Jesus touches the leper. It is completely unusual. Jesus did not fear the disease. Jesus showed compassion and kindness towards the man by touching him with affection and healing. Immediately the man was healed. Jesus commands him to show himself to the priest because it was the next step for him to so that he could return to his family and home.

Luke 5: 12 When He was in a certain city, a man full of leprosy, upon seeing Jesus, fell on his face and begged Him, "Lord, if You will, You can make me clean."

13 He reached out His hand and touched him, saying, "I will. Be clean." And immediately the leprosy left him.

14 Then He commanded him to tell no one, "But go and show yourself to the priest and make an offering for your cleansing, as Moses commanded, as a testimony to them."

Gentleness is not weakness. Meekness is not weakness. Many people may see someone who is meek and gentle as someone who is weak. It isn't true. It takes much strength to do the right thing. An example is that a person should give a soft, gentle reply to someone who is angry. What occurs, is the person has no one to fight with. It quenches strive and avoids it.

Proverbs 15: 1 A soft answer turns away wrath,
    but grievous words stir up anger.

Gentleness is not often thought of as a weapon but it is listed in Psalm 18 as though it is. God's gentleness towards the warrior has strengthened him. Often the comfort of God gives us boldness and courage.

Psalm 18: 35
31 For who is God except the Lord?
    Or who is a rock besides our God?
32 It is God who clothes me with strength,
    and gives my way integrity.
33 He makes my feet like the feet of a deer,
    and causes me to stand on my high places.
34 He trains my hands for war,
    so that my arms bend a bow of bronze.
35 You have given me the shield of Your salvation,
    and Your right hand has held me up,
    and Your gentleness has made me great.
36 You have lengthened my stride under me,
    so that my feet did not slip.

Messiah

The Messiah was prophesied to be as an innocent spotless lamb that would be lead to the slaughter. Messiah would die for the sins of the people. Jesus did not try to defend himself with scripture. He did not fight those who arrested him or who beat him. He did not use any miracle to avoid his death. He could have prayed and thousands of angels could have been released. He endured the suffering so that by his death, burial and resurrection, we could be saved.

Like a lamb to the slaughter opened not his mouth

Isaiah 53: 7 He was oppressed, and he was afflicted,
    yet he opened not his mouth;
he was brought as a lamb to the slaughter,
    and as a sheep before its shearers is silent,
    so he opened not his mouth.

The prophet Jeremiah uses the language of the Messianic prophecy about his own life. He was also unjustly accused and imprisoned.

Jeremiah 11:19 But I was like a gentle lamb that is brought to the slaughter, and I did not know that they had devised plots against me, saying,

The Apostle Paul

The Apostle Paul uses meekness and gentleness as attributes that are highly desirable. They are qualities he uses to describe the agape love of Christ. The following excerpts are his use of the quality as descriptive of a true Christian.

2 Corinthians 10: 1 Now I, Paul, who am lowly in presence among you but bold toward you while absent, appeal to you by the meekness and gentleness of Christ.

Titus 3: 2 Remind them to be subject to rulers and authorities, to obey them, to be ready for every good work, 2 to speak evil of no one, not to be contentious, but gentle, showing all humility toward everyone.

Philippians 4: 5 Let everyone come to know your gentleness. The Lord is at hand.

1 Thessalonians 2: 7 But we were gentle among you, like a nurse caring for her own children. 8 So having great love toward you, we were willing to impart to you not only the gospel of God but also our own lives, because you were dear to us.

1 Timothy 1: 5 Now the goal of this command is love from a pure heart, and from a good conscience, and from sincere faith.
It is a fruit of the Spirit.

Galatians 5: 22 But the fruit of the Spirit is love, joy, peace, patience, gentleness, goodness, faith, 23 meekness, and self-control; against such there is no law. 2

Phil 4:5 Let everyone come to know your gentleness. The Lord is at hand.

7 GOODNESS, RIGHTEOUS

Goodness, Righteous

Goodness and righteousness are the qualities of God that all the saints can declare. God is good. The opposite being evil or corrupt. Good is an essence. All that is good and pure and true comes from God. Before Adam and Eve sinned – they were living in the goodness of God. They could eat from any tree in the garden except the tree of the knowledge of good and evil. Man was never created to know evil. God created us in his image – good. All that is inherently good comes from God. The Psalmist uses the goodness of God as a theme throughout the psalms. The prophets declare that God is good. This chapter will examine the aspects of God's goodness as demonstrated through his righteousness towards us. As spirit filled Christians, we are to have the quality of goodness about us.

The Psalm writer thanks God for mercy. Mercy is good.

Psalm 107: 1 Oh, give thanks unto the Lord, for He is good,
    for His mercy endures forever!

God has delivered us. He is good.

Psalm 107: 2 2 Let the redeemed of the Lord speak out,
    whom He has redeemed from the hand of the enemy,

God led Israel through the desert and provided for her and brought her to the promised land.
God's provision is good.

Psalm 107: 8 Let them praise the Lord for His goodness
    and for His wonderful works to the people!
9 For He satisfies the longing soul
    and fills the hungry soul with goodness.

God faithfully delivered his people. God healed his people. He is good.

Psalm 107: 20 He sent His word and healed them
  and delivered them from their destruction.
21 Let them praise the Lord for His goodness
  and for His wonderful works to the people!
22 And let them offer the sacrifices of thanksgiving
  and declare His works with rejoicing.

The quality of God's constant mercy is good.

Psalm 118: 2 Let Israel say,
  "His mercy endures forever."
3 Let the house of Aaron say,
  "His mercy endures forever."
4 Let those who fear the Lord say,
  "His mercy endures forever."

All of God's attributes are good. All of God's characteristics are good. All of the Spiritual fruit could be acknowledged as good. There is no evil or unrighteousness in Him.

Psalm 92: 15 to show that the Lord is upright;
  He is my rock, and there is no unrighteousness in Him.

Good Shepherd

Jesus explains the quality of the God as the Good Shepherd. He is the good Shepherd, who cares for each of the sheep. Only God is completely good. It is a structural part of his essence. Jesus came to give life and abundant life. This includes caring for all the needs of the sheep. Jesus warns us that the "thief" or enemy (Satan) who comes any other way than through Jesus comes not to bless the sheep but to steal, kill and destroy.

John 10: 7 Then Jesus said to them again, "Truly, truly I say to you, I am the door of the sheep. 8 All who came before Me are thieves and robbers, but the sheep did not listen to them. 9 I am the door. If anyone enters through Me, he will be saved and will go in and out and find pasture. 10 The thief does not come, except to steal and kill and destroy. I came that they may have life, and that they may have it more abundantly.

Jesus used the analogy of a shepherd to describe God's goodness. The people know that the shepherds must carefully watch over their flocks and keep away wolves or bears or lions or thieves. The shepherd may risk his or her life for the sheep. The shepherd cares about the lambs that should be carried rather than left behind. A hireling does the job of a shepherd but does not own the flock. The hireling does not care about the sheep but only desires to get his or her wages. Those who are not owners of the flock may run away should a lion or bear or wolf come.

John 10: 11 "I am the good shepherd. The good shepherd lays down His life for the sheep. 12 But he who is a hired hand, and not a shepherd, who does not own the sheep, sees the wolf coming, and leaves the sheep, and runs away. So the wolf catches the sheep and scatters them. 13 The hired hand runs away because he is a hired hand and does not care about the sheep.

Jesus explains his relationship to the people in terms of a good shepherd. He explains that the shepherd has knowledge of all the sheep and the sheep have knowledge of the shepherd. They come to him because they know and trust the sound of his voice. Jesus explains that he will lay down his life for the sheep and rise up from the dead. Truly this is not understood by his audience until after he rises from the dead. He explains that he willingly gives his life for the sheep. Later this scripture is remembered by his disciples. They understand he is the Messiah would atone for their sins by his own death burial and resurrection..

John 10: 14 "I am the good shepherd. I know My sheep and am known by My own. 15 Even as the Father knows Me, so I know the Father. And I lay down My life for the sheep. 16 I have other sheep who are not of this fold. I must also bring them, and they will hear My voice. There will be one flock and one shepherd. 17 Therefore My Father loves Me, because I lay down My life that I may take it up again. 18 No one takes it from Me, but I lay it down Myself. I have power to lay it down, and I have power to take it up again. I received this command from My Father."

God's word is good, righteous

Because God's loves for us surpasses anything that can be understood except willingness to lay down His life for us so that we can be saved, God's words to us are good. His commandments are right. They are the way of light for us to follow. The commandments and laws of God are given to us to keep us in the way of righteousness. They are given to keep us in a position of receiving blessing, favour and continued prosperity from God. The Psalmist explains the word of God can convert or transform the soul. The word of God can give us wisdom above the wisdom of the earth. The Word of God can give us revelation. In all ways, the Word of God is righteous – good because they are the will of God towards us.

Psalm 19: The law of the Lord is perfect,
   converting the soul;
the testimony of the Lord is sure,
   making wise the simple;
8 the statutes of the Lord are right,
   rejoicing the heart;
the commandment of the Lord is pure,
   enlightening the eyes;
9 the fear of the Lord is clean,
   enduring forever;
the judgments of the Lord are true
   and righteous altogether.

God is just

God cares for all people. Jesus died for all people that whoever will believe on Him will be saved. Many prophets and saints were murdered for their faith unjustly. Because there seemed to be no immediate judgments, it can seem that maybe God didn't make special not of it.
God keeps a record of all things done by all people. God hears the cries of the righteous and sees all things done to them. God will execute judgement for those who were persecuted or those who suffered unjustly. God promises justice.

Luke 18: 7 And shall not God avenge His own elect and be patient with them, who cry day and night to Him? 8 I tell you, He will avenge them speedily.

In the scene in the scripture, there is an outpouring of bowls of wrath onto the earth during God's judgement of the earth. The bowls contain the prayers of all the saints who cried out for justice. Those who were persecuted and martyred are not forgotten. God has their prayers collected. There is a process of collecting of the prayers until the day the bowls are full. It is a day of judgement on the unrighteous or the evil.

Revelation 16: Just true 4 The third angel poured out his bowl on the rivers and springs of water, and they became blood. 5 Then I heard the angel of the waters saying:

"You are righteous, O Lord,
   who is and was and who is to be,

because You have judged these things.
6 For they have shed the blood of saints and prophets,
and You have given them blood to drink. It is what they deserve!"

7 And I heard another from the altar saying:

"Yes, Lord God Almighty,
true and righteous are Your judgments."

Judgement seat of Christ

The throne of Christ is the place all Christians will give account for the lives they lived. Christians will be judged by what we did with the knowledge of Jesus Christ. We are commanded to keep the commission of Christ. We are to bring the good news of Jesus to all people groups in every nation. We are to live our lives holy; we are to do all we can to improve the spheres of influence we have been given. Our words, thought, actions should all align with God's word. Only God is good. God living in us and though us gives a glimpse of Christ to the people in our lives who do not know him.

Revelation 20: 4 I saw thrones, and they sat on them, and the authority to judge was given to them. And I saw the souls of those who had been beheaded for their witness of Jesus and for the word of God. They had not worshipped the beast or his image, and had not received his mark on their foreheads or on their hands. They came to life and reigned with Christ for a thousand years. 5 The rest of the dead did not come to life until the thousand years were ended. This is the first resurrection. 6 Blessed and holy is he who takes part in the first resurrection. Over these the second death has no power, but they shall be priests of God and of Christ and shall reign with Him a thousand years.

Our words and our spiritual fruit or godly character matter.

Matthew 12: 35 A good man out of the good treasure of his heart brings forth good things. And an evil man out of the evil treasure brings forth evil things. 36 But I say to you that for every idle word that men speak, they will give an account on the Day of Judgment. 37 For by your words you will be justified, and by your words you will be condemned."

There is a day of accountability.

2 Corinthians 5: 9 So whether present or absent, we labor that we may be

accepted by Him. 10 For we must all appear before the judgment seat of Christ, that each one may receive his recompense in the body, according to what he has done, whether it was good or bad. Jesus explains that how we treat others determines our true character. It is demonstrated in practical ways such as feeding the hungry or giving water or clothing – literally giving practical things to people who need them. It includes caring for strangers and the sick or those in prison. It involves the God agape love that compels action to bring practical aid to people who are in need. It is described in the parable. Jesus considers no person unworthy of care or of respect. If we are truly living our lives as God would live through us, we will care for all people with God's love so that we in practical ways make a difference in people's lives.

Christians will be judged by what we do or don't do in caring for people (or animals – my emphasis).

Matthew 25: 31 "When the Son of Man comes in His glory, and all the holy angels with Him, then He will sit on the throne of His glory. 32 Before Him will be gathered all nations, and He will separate them one from another as a shepherd separates his sheep from the goats. 33 He will set the sheep at His right hand, but the goats at the left.

34 "Then the King will say to those at His right hand, 'Come, you blessed of My Father, inherit the kingdom prepared for you since the foundation of the world. 35 For I was hungry and you gave Me food, I was thirsty and you gave Me drink, I was a stranger and you took Me in. 36 I was naked and you clothed Me, I was sick and you visited Me, I was in prison and you came to Me.'

37 "Then the righteous will answer Him, 'Lord, when did we see You hungry and feed You, or thirsty and give You drink? 38 When did we see You a stranger and take You in, or naked and clothe You? 39 And when did we see You sick or in prison and come to You?'

40 "The King will answer, 'Truly I say to you, as you have done it for one of the least of these brothers of Mine, you have done it for Me.'

41 "Then He will say to those at the left hand, 'Depart from Me, you cursed, into the eternal fire, prepared for the devil and his angels. 42 For I was hungry and you gave Me no food, I was thirsty and you gave Me no drink, 43 I was a stranger and you did not take Me in, I was naked and you did not clothe Me, I was sick and in prison and you did not visit Me.'

44 "Then they also will answer Him, 'Lord, when did we see You hungry or thirsty or a stranger or naked or sick or in prison, and did not serve You?'

45 "He will answer, 'Truly I say to you, as you did it not for one of the least of these, you did it not for Me.'

46 "And they will go away into eternal punishment, but the righteous into eternal life."

The people all knew the shepherd. Only those who lived a godly life of caring for others received eternal life. What we do towards others, good works because of our true compassionate deeds will be examined by God. All aspects of our lives should show our faith.

The faith of a Christian is necessary; our faith should be demonstrated in good works towards others. We do not do good works to gain favour with God. Once we have repented and received Jesus Christ as our Saviour and Lord, we are saved. We do good works because of our faith. We do good works because we demonstrate our faith through our works.

James 2: 14 What does it profit, my brothers, if a man says he has faith but has no works? Can faith save him? 15 If a brother or sister is naked and lacking daily food, 16 and one of you says to them, "Depart in peace, be warmed and filled," and yet you give them nothing that the body needs, what does it profit? 17 So faith by itself, if it has no works, is dead.

18 But a man may say, "You have faith and I have works."

Show me your faith without your works, and I will show you my faith by my works. 19 You believe that there is one God; you do well. The demons also believe and tremble.

God is light

God is light. Light is symbolized as being good, holy, righteous.

1 John 1: 5 This then is the message which we have heard from Him and declare to you: God is light, and in Him is no darkness at all. 6 If we say that we have fellowship with Him, yet walk in darkness, we lie and do not practice the truth. 7 But if we walk in the light as He is in the light, we have fellowship one with another, and the blood of Jesus Christ His Son cleanses us from all sin.

It is God's Holy Spirit in us that empowers us and compels us to do help those who could never repay us. The light of God lives within us in presence of the Holy Spirit. It is the Holy Spirit who prompts us to give or to serve or to show mercy. It is described in a different passage of scripture as God's light in us. Jesus commands us to shine the light of his goodness throughout the earth.

Matthew 5: 14 "You are the light of the world. A city that is set on a hill cannot be hidden. 15 Neither do men light a candle and put it under a basket, but on a candlestick. And it gives light to all who are in the house. 16 Let your light so shine before men that they may see your good works and glorify your Father who is in heaven.

The White Throne Judgment

The judgement of those who did not know God or receive Jesus as Saviour is a place of eternal judgement with no chance of eternal life with God. Even though it is a place to avoid because of the severity of the judgements, it is just because truly the people themselves did not want God and rejected the provision of Jesus blood. It is a place where unbelieving, wicked people go. It is the destiny of Satan and his demons. It is the place all who reject Jesus Christ will go for eternity.

Revelation 20: 11 Then I saw a great white throne and Him who was seated on it. From His face the earth and the heavens fled away, and no place was found for them. 12 And I saw the dead, small and great, standing before God. Books were opened. Then another book was opened, which is the Book of Life. The dead were judged according to their works as recorded in the books. 13 The sea gave up the dead who were in it, and Death and Hades delivered up the dead who were in them. And they were judged, each one by his works. 14 Then Death and Hades were cast into the lake of fire. This is the second death. 15 Anyone whose name was not found written in the Book of Life was cast into the lake of fire.

Separation from God for eternity is the most horrible thing because God is righteous, good, kind, merciful, compassionate, caring, giving.

It is the reality of the certain judgements to come that compels Christians to give financially towards the gospel. It is the prompt that spurs us to share Christ with people or give a testimony. It is what cause us to pray for people. As long as we are living, we can be sharing Jesus Christ with people. Literally each prayer we pray, God releases blessings toward the people we pray about. Truly angels are released to bring mercy towards people. As we preach and teach Christ or help give to those who do, we are fulfilling Jesus prayer request.

Matthew 9: 36 But when He saw the crowds, He was moved with compassion for them, because they fainted and were scattered, like sheep without a shepherd. 37 Then He said to His disciples, "The harvest truly is plentiful, but the laborers are few. 38 Therefore, pray to the Lord of the harvest, that He will send out laborers into His harvest."

Goodness is the quality of the essence of God that God imparts to Christians. As the Holy Spirit lives on the inside of us, the Holy Spirit is changing us from glory to glory with the character of God. It is the goodness of God that is seen in our words, deeds and lifestyle. It is demonstrated in how we care for the people (and animals – my emphasis) in our spheres of authority.

8 FAITH

Faith,

Faith is substance

Faith is believing in God. Faith is substance; it is spiritual substance. Just as real as a cement post is in the natural, faith is the substance of things hoped for in the spirit realm. It is not seen with the natural eye but it is believed in the spirit man. Faith is the spiritual substance that begins with the human will aligning with God. It requires an expression of human will. The decision is made by each person to believe or not to believe. I have heard preachers call it the currency of heaven. You cannot give or receive anything from God without faith. It is the expression of desire to believe God before any physical evidence is seen.

Hebrews 11: 1 Now faith is the substance of things hoped for, the evidence of things not seen. 2 For by it the men of old obtained a good report.

Come to God with Faith

Before you knew God, it was faith in you searching for the true God. It was faith that came to you by God's mercy to accept Jesus Christ as Saviour. By faith, you say I believe in Jesus. Faith is required for all relationship with God.

John 6: 44 No one can come to Me unless the Father who has sent Me draws him. And I will raise him up on the last day.

Romans 10: 8This is the word of faith that we preach: 9 that if you confess with your mouth Jesus is Lord, and believe in your heart that God has raised Him from the dead, you will be saved, 10 for with the heart one believes unto righteousness, and with the mouth confession is made unto salvation. 11 For the Scripture says, "Whoever believes in Him will not be ashamed."[e] 12 For there is no distinction between Jew and Greek, for the same Lord over all is generous toward all who call upon Him. 13 For, "Everyone who calls on the name of the Lord shall be saved."[f]Measure of faith

Faith required

Hebrews 11:6 And without faith it is impossible to please God, for he who

comes to God must believe that He exists and that He is a rewarder of those who diligently seek Him.
Saved by faith by grace

Ephesians 2: 8 For by grace you have been saved through faith, and this is not of yourselves. It is the gift of God, 9 not of works, so that no one should boast.

Faith Receives

Through faith we receive from God. We receive all things from God by faith. What is not of faith is sin. You may say that is ok for people who have faith but you just don't have any. That is not true.

Every person has a measure of faith. I don't know how much a measure is – because the scripture doesn't emphasize the amount. The scripture emphasizes the existence of faith in all people. What a person does with his faith determines his destiny. Each person must decide to accept Jesus Christ as Saviour by himself. There is no one that can make the decision for you. It is an expression of your human will.

Romans 12: 3 For I say, through the grace given to me, to everyone among you, not to think of himself more highly than he ought to think, but to think with sound judgment, according to the measure of faith God has distributed to every man

Size of your faith

A grain of faith applied can move mountains. Jesus explains that even the smallest amount of faith can produce huge results. He explains that even faith the size of a mustard seed, which is the smallest seed, can move a mountain. It is an analogy of faith being such a mighty particle it can affect the natural realm in a mighty way – in what we would term as miracles or things that supersede the laws of science and technology.

It should bring encouragement to us. We can affect our spheres of influence with even a grain or seed of faith. A mustard seed is tiny but when it is planted and watered, it grows. Faith is something that can increase as well.

Matthew 17: 20 Jesus said to them, "Because of your unbelief. For truly I say to you, if you have faith as a grain of mustard seed, you will say to this mountain, 'Move from here to there,' and it will move. And nothing will be impossible for you. 21 But this kind does not go out except by prayer and fasting."

Gift of faith

All people have a measure of faith. Some people have been given a special gift of faith. It is usually manifest in the working of miracles or gifts of healings. They may be Apostles, Prophets, Evangelists. It is special faith for special miracles or special answers to prayer.

I have seen the manifestation of the gift of faith in healing evangelists, apostles and prophets with signs and wonders following. That is that men, women and children received their healing or deliverance. People received answers to prayer. My pastor believed for finances way beyond what the church could afford to purchase a plot of land. He knew that God had spoken to him so he agreed to meet the real estate dealer and bring the money. Up until that very day, all the money expected had not come in; finally, within an hour or two of the meeting, the pastor received the remaining funds by members of the congregation.

Romans 12: 4 For just as we have many parts in one body, and not all parts have the same function, 5 so we, being many, are one body in Christ, and all are parts of one another. 6 We have diverse gifts according to the grace that is given to us: if prophecy, according to the proportion of faith; 7 if service, in serving; he who teaches, in teaching; 8 he who exhorts, in exhortation; he who gives, with generosity; he who rules, with diligence; he who shows mercy, with cheerfulness.

Faith Grows

Faith is as a seed. It must be planted. You may wonder about this analogy. A seed must be planted in the earth for it to grow. I am fascinated by the seeds that are found that are thousands of years old and planted and grow. A seed is the essence of the thing that you want. For example, I am a gardener. I would like a crop of lettuce, I must plant lettuce seeds. I can plant radish seeds to get radishes. I can plant cucumber seed to get cucumbers. It begins with one seed.

Physical seed is planted in the earth. Spiritual seed (the substance of things hoped for or the essence of what you desire) is planted in the spirit with a decision of your human will coming into alignment with God's word. If it isn't something that aligns with God's word, you cannot believe that God will give it to you because He never contradicts His word. God's

Word is His expressed will for our lives. You believe God and you thank Him for it. The best way to do it is to read the scriptures and get God to quicken a scripture or series of scriptures to you. All things concerning our lives as humans is in the word of God. In the parable of the sower Jesus describes different types of soils the seed is sown it that determine its productivity.

Matthew 13: 3 Then He told them many things in parables, saying, "Listen! A sower went out to sow. 4 While he sowed, some seeds fell beside the path, and the birds came and devoured them. 5 But other seeds fell on rocky ground where they did not have much soil, and immediately they sprang up because they did not have deep soil. 6 But when the sun rose, they were scorched. And because they did not take root, they withered away. 7 Some seeds fell among thorns, and the thorns grew up and choked them. 8 But other seeds fell into good ground and produced grain: a hundred, sixty, or thirty times as much. 9 Whoever has ears to hear, let him hear."

Just as the soil affects the harvest of 30-fold, 60-fold or 100-fold, our heart affects the effectiveness of our faith. I don't mean the literal heart organ in your body. I mean the center of your being – a living spirit that has a soul that lives in your body. How you maintain your heart determines the productivity of the seed sown.

Soil affects seed growth

Never plant a seed in rocky soil. If you are not sure it is God's will – don't sow. Instead research the scriptures. If you are worried, it is unbelief – don't sow - like the weeds and thorns; get hold of your will and speak the Word of God to yourself and over yourself so that you come into alignment with God's Word Afterwards, sow in faith. Once you know it is in God's Word and His will for us is expressed in God's Word, plant the seed in the good soil of your heart.

Pray it because you know it is in God's will. Believe it as you pray, knowing it is God's pleasure to give you the kingdom. He delights in the prosperity of his servant. Know that God is good; He is merciful and He cares about you. Thank God for releasing angels to perform it. Thank God for the answer. Literally say "Thank you God I receive it." Say it in faith and believe it. Start praising God for it. Each day thank God for it. If it is a thing, get a picture of it and hang it in a place where you will see it to remind yourself that your miracle is on the way. As you see it, thank God for your miracle. Your words must align with what you are believing God for. Faith such as described is in good soil to produce 100-fold.

Matthew 13: 18 "Therefore listen to the parable of the sower. 19 When anyone hears the word of the kingdom and does not understand it, the evil one comes and snatches away what was sown in his heart. This is the one who received seed beside the path. 20 But he who received the seed on rocky ground is he who hears the word and immediately receives it with joy, 21 yet he has no root in himself, but endures for a while. For when tribulation or persecution arises because of the word, eventually he falls away. 22 He also who received seed among the thorns is he who hears the word, but the cares of this world and the deceitfulness of riches choke the word, and he becomes unfruitful. 23 But he who received seed on the good ground is he who hears the word and understands it, who indeed bears fruit. Some produce a hundred, sixty, or thirty times what was sown."

Mustard Seed Grows into a Tree

In a different excerpt Jesus explains how a tiny seed grows into a huge tree that can shelter birds. The growth of the tiny seed into a huge tree is emphasized.

Matthew 13: 31 He told them another parable, saying, "The kingdom of heaven is like a grain of mustard seed which a man took and sowed in his field. 32 This indeed is the least of all seeds, but when it has grown, it is the greatest among herbs and is a tree, so that the birds of the air come and lodge in its branches."

Growing your faith

Even though you may plant your faith, that is as a tiny seed, it will grow. Physical plants require sun and water to grow. Spiritual faith grows by hearing God's Word. I like what Gloria Copeland said, "faith comes by hearing and hearing" She emphasized that part of the scripture to emphasize the need to keep hearing God's Word over and over. The more we hear the promise of God we are believing for, the more it will encourage our faith to grow. Each time we hear it, we should come into agreement with it and thank God for the answer to prayer.

Faith comes by hearing and hearing by the word of God

Romans 10: 16 But they have not all obeyed the gospel. For Isaiah says, "Lord, who has believed our report?"[h] 17 So then faith comes by hearing, and hearing by the word of God.

Faith and Patience Inherit Promises

We require faith and patience to inherit the promises. Faith is necessary but so is patience. We must be consistent in our prayers and thanking of God by faith for the answer. We must not speak words of doubt or unbelief. Our words should align with God's Word.

Hebrews 6: 11 We desire that every one of you show the same diligence for the full assurance of hope to the end, 12 so that you may not be lazy, but imitators of those who through faith and patience inherit the promises.

Faith in God's Word

Three virtues are described in scripture. Faith, hope and love. They are important to our spiritual life.

1 Corinthians 13: 13 So now abide faith, hope, and love, these three. But the greatest of these is love.

Your Faith

Faith in Jesus Christ as healer is evidenced throughout the new testament. Faith is necessary to receive healing from God. It can be your faith; it can be the person ministering's faith; it can be someone else's faith. There were several people out of the multitudes that Jesus heals that were noted in the scripture for faith.

The woman with the issue of blood is especially noted. She has been hemorrhaging for 12 long years. She gave all she had to different types of cures but found no answer. She heard about Jesus and the miracles he did and believed in her heart. She made a decision. She planted her faith. She believed, if I can only touch the edge of his garment, I can be healed. I've heard much preaching on these scriptures.

I like the explanation of the woman needing to be on the ground to touch the hem of his robe. She had to kneel in a crowd of people and reach to touch the hem of his robe. There were hundreds of people there all hoping to see Jesus. All types of people were brushing up against him but her touch was different. Hers was a touch of faith. As soon as she touched the hem of his garment she stopped bleeding. She was made whole. Jesus felt virtue flow from him. What that means is he felt the faith reach towards him for a miracle. He stopped and said it out loud. She confessed that it was her. Jesus spoke to her "Daughter, your faith has made you whole."

Mark 5: And many people followed Him and pressed in on Him. 25 And a certain woman had a hemorrhage for twelve years, 26 and had suffered much under many physicians. She had spent all that she had, and was not better but rather grew worse. 27 When she had heard of Jesus, she came in the crowd behind Him and touched His garment. 28 For she said, "If I may touch His garments, I shall be healed." 29 And immediately her hemorrhage dried up, and she felt in her body that she was healed of the affliction.

30 At once, Jesus knew within Himself that power had gone out of Him. He turned around in the crowd and said, "Who touched My garments?"

31 His disciples said to Him, "You see the crowd pressing against You, and You say, 'Who touched Me?' "

32 And He looked around to see her who had done it. 33 But the woman, fearing and trembling, knowing what had happened to her, came and fell down before Him and told Him the entire truth. 34 He said to her, "Daughter, your faith has made you well. Go in peace, and be healed of your affliction."

Healing of the Roman Centurion's Servant

Romans certainly were not openly following Jesus around listening to his preaching. However, one centurion heard of Jesus somehow and went to see him because his servant that he loved was ill. The centurion spoke words that astounded Jesus. Jesus was willing to go heal the servant. The centurion recognized that Jesus had spiritual authority and believed that Jesus could speak the word only and it would be done. He asked for Jesus to heal his servant.

The scriptures say, "Jesus marveled at his faith" Jesus saw faith in a Gentile and said he had not encountered anyone else with such faith.

Luke 7: 7 When He had completed all His words in the hearing of the people, He entered Capernaum. 2 Now a centurion's[a] servant, who was dear to him, was sick and ready to die. 3 When he heard of Jesus, he sent the elders of the Jews to Him, asking Him to come and heal his servant. 4 When they came to Jesus, they asked Him earnestly, saying, "You should do this for him for he is worthy, 5 for he loves our nation, and he has built us a synagogue." 6 So Jesus went with them.

When He was not far from the house, the centurion sent friends to Him, saying, "Lord, do not trouble Yourself, for I am not worthy to have You come under my roof. 7 Likewise, I did not think myself worthy to come to You. But say the word, and my servant will be healed. 8 For I myself am a man placed under authority, having soldiers under me. I say to one, 'Go,' and he goes, and to another, 'Come,' and he comes, and to my servant, 'Do this,' and he does it."

As the centurion went on his way, his servants came confirming that at the very moment that Jesus spoke it the servant was healed.

Luke 7: 9 When Jesus heard these words, He marveled at him, and turned and said to the people who followed Him, "I tell you, I have not found such great faith even in Israel." 10 Then those who were sent, returning to the house, found the servant well who had been sick.

Healing Faith

Blind men who heard about Jesus healing people cried out in faith for Jesus to have mercy on them. They appealed to him as "son of David" rather than Jesus. They were aligning themselves with the faith to believe Jesus was the promised Messiah through the lineage of David. Jesus asked them a direct faith question. "Do you believe I am able to do it?" They confessed with their mouths – "yes LORD" and they received healing. Jesus spoke to them these words: "According to your faith, let it be done unto you." That is a positive word of encouragement to those who believe. It means their faith has a part in the healing. They believed; they received.

Matthew 9: 27 As Jesus departed from there, two blind men followed Him, crying out and saying, "Son of David, have mercy on us!"

28 When He entered the house, the blind men came to Him. And Jesus said to them, "Do you believe that I am able to do this?"

They said to Him, "Yes, Lord."

29 Then He touched their eyes, saying, "According to your faith, let it be done for you." 30 And their eyes were opened, and Jesus strictly commanded them, saying, "See that no one knows of it." 31 But when they had departed, they spread His fame in all that region

Faith Giant: Abraham

Abraham is one of the many listed in the 11th chapter of Hebrews as a hero of faith. Truly, Abraham dwelt among idol worshippers. God spoke to him and Abraham believed God. It took radical obedience. Abraham left his family and all he knew to go to a place that God would show him. He and his wife did not have any children and they were in their 70's, but God promised to bless them with children as many as the stars in the sky or grains of sand on the ground. It is a huge thing that God promised Abram. It took 30 years for the manifestation of the miracle. Finally, Abraham had children and God showed him the promised land. God spoke to him about the future of his descendants.

Hebrews 11: 8 By faith Abraham obeyed when he was called to go out into a place which he would later receive as an inheritance. He went out not knowing where he was going. 9 By faith he dwelt in the promised land, as in a foreign land, dwelling in tents with Isaac and Jacob, the heirs of the same promise, 10 for he was looking for a city which has foundations, whose builder and maker is God. 11 By faith Sarah herself also received the ability to conceive seed, and she bore a child when she was past the age, because she judged Him faithful who had promised. 12 Therefore from one man, who was as good as dead, sprang so many, a multitude as the stars of the sky and innumerable as the sand by the seashore.

It took faith to believe that he heard from God. It took faith for him to leave his home and all within his family. It took faith for him to persist even though there was no visible sign of the promise for 30 years. Abraham believed God could call those things that be not as though they were. It explains concisely. Speak or call those things that you desire to be that they would be manifest even though you don't yet see them.

Romans 4: 16 Therefore the promise comes through faith, so that it might be by grace, that the promise would be certain to all the descendants, not only to those who are of the law, but also to those who are of the faith of Abraham, who is the father of us all 17 (as it is written, "I have made you a father of many nations"[c]) before God whom he believed, and who raises the dead, and calls those things that do not exist as though they did.

Believed God

Because Abraham believed God, Abraham received the promise. His faith was considered righteous by God.

Romans 4: 19 And not being weak in faith, he did not consider his own body to be dead (when he was about a hundred years old), nor yet the deadness of Sarah's womb. 20 He did not waver at the promise of God through unbelief, but was strong in faith, giving glory to God, 21 and being fully persuaded that what God had promised, He was able to perform. 22 Therefore "it was credited to him as righteousness.

Living Faith

God's Word can be engrafted into your soul. What that means in terms of our study is that if you are lacking anything, God's word is the provision of it. As you plant the scripture into your heart by praying it and saying it, and aligning your life with it, the word becomes a part of you. I have grafted several plants and trees. A branch that has the flowers on it. Ban be grafted into a tree that doesn't have flowers and it can start producing flowers. The Word of God engrafted into your heart can start producing the fruit of God's Word in your life. The engrafted word can transform your life. The engrafted word can save your soul.

James 1: 21 Therefore lay aside all filthiness and remaining wickedness and receive with meekness the engrafted word, which is able to save your souls.

Hearing the word is necessary for faith to arise, but there should also be a keeping of the word in alignment with your life style: the scripture says it is a doing of the word.

James 1:22 Be doers of the word and not hearers only, deceiving yourselves. 23 For if anyone is a hearer of the word and not a doer, he is like a man viewing his natural face in a mirror. 24 He views himself, and goes his way, and immediately forgets what kind of man he was. 25 But whoever looks into the perfect law of liberty, and continues in it, and is not a forgetful hearer but a doer of the work, this man will be blessed in his deeds.

Faith is demonstrated by our words, thoughts, actions

James 2: 14 What does it profit, my brothers, if a man says he has faith but has no works? Can faith save him? 15 If a brother or sister is naked and lacking daily food, 16 and one of you says to them, "Depart in peace, be warmed and filled," and yet you give them nothing that the body needs, what does it profit? 17 So faith by itself, if it has no works, is dead.

18 But a man may say, "You have faith and I have works."
Show me your faith without your works, and I will show you my faith by

my works. 19 You believe that there is one God; you do well. The demons also believe and tremble.

Faith of a child

The disciples were with Jesus and were competing with each other and measuring each other against each other to see who was the best disciple. Jesus saw them striving to prove who was most important and stopped it right at that point. Jesus showed them the children who gathered around Jesus because he was kind, gentle and loving. He pointed to their humility and simplicity to correct them from jealousy and pride.

The children's faith in Jesus was innocent. Jesus said that is the disciples would humble themselves as children, they would truly be most noteworthy. In the kingdom of God, he that serves is higher than he who commands. Jesus proved this truth and sealed it with his blood by dying for our sins.

Matthew 18: 18 At that time the disciples came to Jesus, saying, "Who is the greatest in the kingdom of heaven?"

2 Jesus called a little child to Him and set him in their midst, 3 and said, "Truly I say to you, unless you are converted and become like little children, you will not enter the kingdom of heaven. 4 Therefore whoever humbles himself like this little child is greatest in the kingdom of heaven. 5 And whoever receives one such little child in My name receives Me.

Faith of Thomas

Jesus revealed himself to the disciples after his resurrection from the dead. They saw him and had dinner with him. Thomas was not there with them. When they told him of Jesus appearance, Thomas did not believe. In fact, he made a condition for believing. It was a prove it to me type of statement. He wanted to see the nail prints himself and place his fingers in the wounds or he would not believe. This type of demand shows a very weak kind of faith. Jesus appeared to him knowing what Thomas had said and Jesus specifically told Thomas to place his fingers in Jesus' wounds so that he could know it was Jesus. Thomas realizes it is truly Jesus.

John 20: 24 But Thomas, one of the twelve, called The Twin, was not with them when Jesus came. 25 So the other disciples told him, "We have seen the Lord!"

But he said to them, "Unless I see the nail prints in His hands, and put my finger in the nail prints, and put my hand in His side, I will not believe."

John 20: 26 After eight days His disciples were again inside with the doors shut, and Thomas was with them. Jesus came and stood among them, and said, "Peace be with you." 27 Then He said to Thomas, "Put your finger here, and look at My hands. Put your hand here and place it in My side. Do not be faithless, but believing."

28 Thomas answered Him, "My Lord and my God!"

29 Jesus said to him, "Thomas, because you have seen Me, you have believed. Blessed are those who have not seen, and have yet believed."

Jesus does not condemn him for his unbelief and truly shows his wounds and nail prints. Jesus says that those who have not seen but believe have the most faith. He also encourages his to be believing rather than faithless.

God's Word

God's faith creates as He speaks. Whatever God says always comes to pass. That is how all things were created by God's Word. It is through faith in God's written word that we come into agreement with God and speak what God's will is. It brings it to come to pass.

God spoke and all things were created. His Words have creative potential to bring about the very thing he speaks.

Genesis 1: 3 God said, "Let there be light," and there was light.

God gave Adam the authority to name all the animals. It is the creative power to speak and have dominion over all the earth God gave to humans.

Genesis 2: 19 Out of the ground the Lord God formed every beast of the field and every bird of the sky, and brought them to the man to see what he would call them. Whatever the man called every living creature, that was its name. 20 The man gave names to all the livestock, to the birds of the sky, and to every beast of the field, but for Adam[c] there was not found a helper suitable for him.

God's word always accomplishes what it is sent to do. As we align with God's Word, we believe in the promises God has given us through scripture. Faith in God's Word quickens the Word to the human spirit and releases supernatural dynamics to cause the Word to come to pass.

Isaiah 55: 10 For as the rain comes down,
  and the snow from heaven,
and do not return there
  but water the earth
and make it bring forth and bud
  that it may give seed to the sower and bread to the eater,
11 so shall My word be that goes forth from My mouth;
  it shall not return to Me void,
but it shall accomplish that which I please,
  and it shall prosper in the thing for which I sent it.

As we believe, so should we speak that our words would align with God's Word. Our confession of faith, is saying what God's Word teaches.

2 Corinthians 4: 13 We have the same spirit of faith. As it is written, "I believed, and therefore I have spoken."[a] So we also believe and therefore speak, 14 knowing that He who raised the Lord Jesus will also raise us through Jesus and will present us with you.
Faith compels a person to speak life

If we want to see the miracles of God manifest in our lives, we must believe in and speak the Word of God. God is Spirit; by aligning our human wills with God's word, we align with God and His will. Faith is necessary for all relationship with God and for all giving and receiving from God.

If you want to improve your giving and receiving from God, examine your words. Our words must align with God's Word. We cannot be speaking things such as "I don't believe" and expect to receive anything from God. We cannot grumble or complain or be in strife. Words are important as is our attitude as they indicate our alignment with God. Pray asking the Holy Spirit to set a watch over your words so that if you speak anything out of God's will, the Holy Spirit will correct you. Should you do it, expect God to answer you.

9 SELF CONTROL, TEMPERANCE

Self-Control; Temperance

Galatians 5: 23 meekness, and self-control; against such there is no law.

Temperance or self-control is the ability to live holy and wisely in the earth. It involves prudence, wisdom, discerning of spirits, faith and much more. It is not just a natural ability; it is spiritual fruit. Spiritual fruit grows by the word of God and presence in God's presence. The scriptures give us many references to self-control or temperance. Keeping one's heart right is essential to getting wisdom and to living a temperate life.

Keeping right with God

Proverbs 4: 23 Keep your heart with all diligence,
    for out of it are the issues of life.

Keeping the heart

Keeping the heart pure is necessary to have self- control or to receive anything from God.

As Adam and Eve were responsible for keeping the garden of Eden, so are we responsible to keep our hearts. There were no weeds or thorns in the garden of Eden. The trees were bearing fruit and all they had to do is pick the fruit they wanted. They did have one warning though. They were to not eat from the tree of the knowledge of good and evil. They had to keep God's commandment. It is not simply the action of disobeying God that was the sin they committed. They committed spiritual blasphemy by partaking of the fruit of the tree of the knowledge of good and evil.

Satan possessed the serpent and seduced Eve and Adam with her, to disobey God.
First, he twisted God's word by asking them if God let them eat from any of trees in the garden.

Genesis 3: 3 Now the serpent was more subtle than any beast of the field which the Lord God had made. And he said to the woman, "Has God said, 'You shall not eat of any tree of the garden'?"

Eve responded to the serpent with a twist of the truth. She said they could not eat from the tree of the knowledge of good and evil. She added they shouldn't even touch it. She twisted the truth.

Genesis 3: 2 And the woman said to the serpent, "We may eat of the fruit from the trees of the garden; 3 but from the fruit of the tree which is in the midst of the garden, God has said, 'You will not eat of it, nor will you touch it, or else you will die.'"

Satan spoke through the serpent again adding words doubting God's commandment. He first told them God was not speaking the truth; they would not die. Secondly, he spoke saying the fruit would make them as gods knowing good from evil.

Genesis 3: 4 Then the serpent said to the woman, "You surely will not die! 5 For God knows that on the day you eat of it your eyes will be opened and you will be like God, knowing good and evil."

It was at that point, the serpent possessed by Satan had caught her in his trap.

1 John 2: 16 For all that is in the world—the lust of the flesh, the lust of the eyes, and the pride of life—is not of the Father, but is of the world. 17 The world and its desires are passing away, but the one who does the will of God lives forever.

She began to lust after its flesh. It was a lust of seeing something she not have. She saw the tree was good for fruit. She desired it because she wanted to be as wise as a god (promise of Satan). She was filled with pride. The lusts of the devil are the same traps he uses against us.

Genesis 3: 6 When the woman saw that the tree was good for food, that it was pleasing to the eyes and a tree desirable to make one wise, she took of its fruit and ate; and she gave to her husband with her, and he ate. 7 Then the eyes of both were opened, and they knew that they were naked. So they sewed fig leaves together and made coverings for themselves.

Not only did Eve partake of it but she gave some to Adam who was there with her and said nothing. Immediately they died spiritually in their holy innocence with God. They knew they were naked. They felt shame. They were afraid of God. They felt fear. These things are the knowledge of evil. God never intended for Adam and Eve to know sin or the consequences of it. They willfully chose to disobey God.

Adam and Eve sinned by increments. Their hearts were drawn to sin by the devil's clever schemes. A person who would like to live in temperance or self-control must guard his or her heart. Guarding the heart is not a list of rules. It is obedience to the Holy Spirit who lives in us. What comes into the heart of a person comes through the eyes and ears. It is what we listen to, what we read, what we watch and how we allow things into our heart that determines if we will guard our heart.

Your heart can be right, only if you follow the leading of the Holy Spirit. Seriously commit your life fresh and pray "Holy Spirit please let me only receive things that are pure and aligning with God's word in my life." If you truly commit yourself in that way, the Holy Spirit will prompt you. You may realize the music you are listening to contains words that should not be going into your ears. You may realize the tv shows you watch or the movies you enjoy are not pleasing to God. I am only talking about in your sphere of influence.

What you partake of you can control; only receive what is pleasing to God. Sure, there will be things in society that don't align with God's Word, as I say it I tremble to admit it. What we directly seek and partake of influences our life. Guarding the heart would be to first become aware of what we allow and next to obey the Holy Spirit and replace our habits with spiritual, healthy alternatives.

These scriptures are cautions to keep the heart pure without sin.

What we allow in our lives will establish our thinking and ideals.

Proverbs 16: 3 Commit your works to the Lord,
   and your thoughts will be established.

Pride will always contaminate anything you do if you do not root it out.
Proverbs 16: 19 Better it is to be of a humble spirit with the lowly
   than to divide the spoil with the proud.

Proverbs 18: 12 Before destruction the heart of man is haughty,
   and before honor is humility.

Proverbs 21: 4 A high look, a proud heart,
   and the plowing of the wicked are sin.

Life or Death

The words of our mouth can speak life or death. Our words should be used with wisdom. Once you say something, you can never take it back again. It is possible that your words could wound someone. You can pray for forgiveness, but the stinger has already made the wound. Yes, God can heal people, but it is best not to attack people with words.

Proverbs 18: 21 Death and life are in the power of the tongue,
    and those who love it will eat its fruit.

Proverbs 19: 1 Better is the poor who walks in his integrity
    than he who is perverse in his lips and is a fool.

Proverbs 20: 15 There is gold and a multitude of rubies,
    but the lips of knowledge are a precious jewel.

Keep your own spirit

Proverbs 23: 23 Buy the truth, and do not sell it,
    also wisdom and instruction and understanding.

Proverbs 25: 28 He who has no rule over his own spirit
    is like a city that is broken down and without walls.

Proverbs 29: 20 Do you see a man who is hasty in his words?
    There is more hope for a fool than for him.

Warning about immoral relationships

Proverbs 5: 3 For the lips of an immoral woman drip as a honeycomb,
    and her mouth is smoother than oil.
4 But her end is bitter as wormwood,
    sharp as a two-edged sword.
5 Her feet go down to death,
    her steps take hold of Sheol.
6 She does not ponder the path of life;
    her ways are unstable, and she does not know it.

Proverbs 23: 27 For a prostitute is a deep ditch,
    and a seductress is a narrow pit.

Concerning food

Proverbs 25: 16 Have you found honey? Eat only as much as is sufficient for you,
    lest you be filled with it and vomit it.

Proverbs 25: 27 It is not good to eat much honey;
    so for men to search their own glory is not glory.

1 Corinthians 6: 10 nor thieves, nor covetous, nor drunkards, nor revilers, nor extortioners will inherit the kingdom of God.

Concerning Words

Proverbs 12: 13 The wicked is snared by the transgression of his lips,
    but the just will come out of trouble.

14 A man will be satisfied with good by the fruit of his mouth,
    and the recompense of a man's hands will be rendered to him.

Proverbs 15: 2 The tongue of the wise uses knowledge aright,
    but the mouth of fools pours out foolishness.

Proverbs 16: 16 How much better to get wisdom than gold!
    And to get understanding is to be chosen rather than silver!

Concerning Anger

Proverbs 14: 17 He who is quick-tempered deals foolishly, and a man of wicked devices is hated.

Proverbs 15: 18 A wrathful man stirs up strife,
    but he who is slow to anger appeases strife.
Concerning company
Proverbs 25: 17 Withdraw your foot from your neighbor's house,
    lest he be weary of you and so hate you.

Love of money

Proverbs 15: 16 Better is little with the fear of the Lord
    than great treasure with trouble.

Proverbs 16: 8 Better is a little with righteousness

than great revenues with injustice.
Concerning relationships

Proverbs 16: 28 A perverse man sows strife,
 and a whisperer separates the best of friends.

Proverbs 16: 32 He who is slow to anger is better than the mighty,
 and he who rules his spirit than he who takes a city.

Dealing with money

Proverbs 21: 20 There is treasure to be desired and oil in the dwelling of the wise,
 but a foolish man squanders it.

Covetousness

Proverbs 21: 25 The desire of the slothful kills him,
 for his hands refuse to labor.
26 He covets greedily all the day long,
 but the righteous gives and does not spare.

Proverbs 28: 6 Better is the poor who walks in his uprightness
 than he who is perverse in his ways, though he be rich.

Proverbs 27: 20 Death and destruction are never full;
 so the eyes of man are never satisfied.

Proverbs 28: 20 A faithful man will abound with blessings,
 but he who makes haste to be rich will not be innocent.

Not given to wine

While discussing the requirements for elders in the church, the Apostle Paul lists character qualities that are important. He does not emphasize spiritual gifts, or Charisma. He emphasizes spiritual fruit. The requirements describe a person who is wholly given to God with the Holy Spirit leading the person's life. Drinking wine is not a sin, but being drunk is. Being self-controlled is one of the strong requirements. The person must be respectable within the church and from in the community. The person should be able to teach.

1 Timothy 3: 2 An overseer then must be blameless, the husband of one

wife, sober, self-controlled, respectable, hospitable, able to teach; 3 not given to drunkenness, not violent, not greedy for money, but patient, not argumentative, not covetous; 4 and one who manages his own house well, having his children in submission with all reverence.

1 Timothy 3: 7 Moreover he must have a good reputation among those who are outsiders, so that he does not fall into reproach and the snare of the devil.

1 Timothy 3: 8 Likewise deacons must be serious, not insincere, not given to much wine, not greedy, 9 keeping the mystery of the faith in a pure conscience. 10 And let them first be tested; then, being found blameless, let them serve as deacons.

11 Likewise, their wives must be serious, not slanderers, sober, and faithful in all things.

Prosperity – God's will

Some people believe that the Bible says money is the root of all sin but it doesn't. Money, wealth and riches are not an indication of sin. It depends upon the person's heart. If God is the priority in your life, you will not worship money. It is God's desire to prosper his people. That includes finances, health, and all aspects of life. God will meet your needs but he will also give you the desires of your heart. O yes. There is a catch; you must keep your heart right with God. A person who delights in God will worship God and honour God in all areas of life, including money.

God desires to give all things you need and even desire.

Psalm 37: 4 Delight yourself in the Lord,
    and He will give you the desires of your heart.

Jesus tells us that all these things we need will be added unto us if we will seek God first. Whatever we fix our hearts on, will become our God. Guarding the heart has to do with keeping god's Word but also Keeping our relationship with God as a priority.

Luke 12: 31 But seek the kingdom of God, and all these things shall be given to you.

Luke 12: 32 "Do not be afraid, little flock, for it is your Father's good pleasure to give you the kingdom. 33 Sell your possessions and give alms.

Provide yourselves purses that do not grow old, an unfailing treasure in the heavens, where no thief comes near and no moth destroys. 34 For where your treasure is, there will your heart be also.

Philippians 4: 19 But my God shall supply your every need according to His riches in glory by Christ Jesus.

God's promises to Moses and Israel is that He would most surely prosper and bless them if they would keep the commandments.

Deuteronomy 28: 8 The Lord will command the blessing on you in your barns and in all that you set your hand to do, and He will bless you in the land which the Lord your God is giving you.

9 The Lord will establish you as a holy people to Himself, just as He swore to you, if you will keep the commandments of the Lord your God and walk in His ways. 10 All people of the earth shall see that you are called by the name of the Lord, and they shall be afraid of you. 11 The Lord will make you overflow in prosperity, in the offspring of your body, in the offspring of your livestock, and in the produce of your ground, in the land which the Lord swore to your fathers to give you.

12 The Lord will open up to you His good treasure, the heavens, to give the rain to your land in its season and to bless all the work of your hand. You will lend to many nations, but you will not borrow. 13 The Lord will make you the head and not the tail; you will only be above and you will not be beneath, if you listen to the commandments of the Lord your God, which I am commanding you today, to observe and to do them. 14 Also, you shall not turn aside from any of the words which I am commanding you today, to the right hand or to the left, to go after other gods to serve them.

There is a warning about the love of money. What it means is that money and wealth has become your god. You use people, you may even use God, to acquire money and wealth. It is a spirit of covetousness. It is an indication of someone who is committing adultery against God. God wants to bless us financially so we can spread the gospel all over the earth. God wants to bless us so we can help other people. The more we have, the more we can give. We can help people that others cannot.

Love of Money

1 Timothy 6: 9 But those who desire to be rich fall into temptation and a snare and into many foolish and harmful lusts, which drown men in ruin

and destruction. 10 For the love of money is the root of all evil. While coveting after money, some have strayed from the faith and pierced themselves through with many sorrows.

The Apostle Paul encourages Timothy to follow God with all his being. It involves following righteousness, godliness, faith, love, patience, and gentleness all Spiritual fruit. It is godly character that can strengthen you to live a life wholly and holy to God. As much as I thank God for Spiritual gifts and as much I desire the gifts of the Spirit, temperance is something that is within the inner most character. It can only come as we are in God's presence, praying, worshipping, giving serving, living one day after another with God as our focus. As we honour God, we are transformed form glory to glory in terms of our character. Spiritual fruit grows as we live in communion with God.

Spiritual gifts can be imparted to others. Spiritual fruit only God can grow. Our hearts must be yielded to Him.

Godly character

We should yield ourselves unto God praying that God will changes us from glory to glory. Continual coming to God, yielding of our lives unto the Holy Spirit will see transformation of our lives.

1 Timothy 6: 11 But you, O man of God, escape these things, and follow after righteousness, godliness, faith, love, patience, and gentleness. 12 Fight the good fight of faith. Lay hold on eternal life, to which you are called and have professed a good profession before many witnesses. 13 I command you, in the sight of God, who gives life to all things, and in the sight of Christ Jesus, who testified a good confession before Pontius Pilate, 14 to keep this commandment without blemish, blameless until the appearing of our Lord Jesus Christ, 15 which He, who is the blessed and only Ruler, the King of kings and Lord of lords, will reveal at the proper time. 16 He alone has immortality, living in unapproachable light, whom no one has seen, nor can see. To Him be honor and everlasting power. Amen.

The Apostle Paul

The Apostle Paul was preaching freedom to Gentiles – the freedom of Jesus Christ. He was not making the Gentiles become Jews first and then converting them to Jesus as Messiah. He was directly leading them to believe in Jesus to be saved. Paul explains his freedom from the law by explaining that all although he could do all things, he will not be in bondage to any of them. He is making a statement of temperance. He is saying he will to be addicted to anything. He strictly forbids sex outside of marriage explaining that although he is free from keeping the law to be saved, he must keep the commandments of God.

1 Corinthians 6: 12 "All things are lawful to me," but not all things are helpful. "All things are lawful for me," but I will not be brought under the power of anything. 13 "Food is for the belly, and the belly is for food," but God will destroy both of them. Now the body is not for sexual immorality, but for the Lord, and the Lord is for the body. 14 God has raised up the Lord and will also raise us up by His own power. 15 Do you not know that your bodies are the parts of Christ? Shall I then take the parts of Christ and make them the parts of a harlot? God forbid! 16 What? Do you not know that he who is joined to a harlot is one body with her? For "the two," He says, "shall become one flesh."[a] 17 But he who is joined to the Lord becomes one spirit with Him.

The sin of adultery affects a person's body, soul and spirit.

1 Corinthians 6: 18 Escape from sexual immorality. Every sin that a man commits is outside the body. But he who commits sexual immorality sins against his own body. 19 What? Do you not know that your body is the temple of the Holy Spirit, who is in you, whom you have received from God, and that you are not your own? 20 You were bought with a price. Therefore, glorify God in your body and in your spirit, which are God's.

Hebrews 13: Marriage is to be honored among everyone, and the bed undefiled. But God will judge the sexually immoral and adulterers. 5 Let your lives be without love of money, and be content with the things you have. For He has said:

"I will never leave you,
  nor forsake you."[a]

The Apostle Paul speaks to warn the people of the snares of sin and iniquity. being sober, doesn't simply mean not getting drunk, it also means being observant and remembering that although we are on the earth in physical bodies, there is a spiritual aspect to our lives and that we cannot forget the devil is our enemy. We must be on guard. It is not to frighten us but to cause to pray and to make decisions wisely.

Be Sober be Vigilant

1 Peter 5: 8 Be sober and watchful, because your adversary the devil walks around as a roaring lion, seeking whom he may devour. 9 Resist him firmly in the faith, knowing that the same afflictions are experienced by your brotherhood throughout the world.

Again, in the passage below the apostle Paul is speaking that the people we wise. It has to do with pursuing God rather than mere food and drink. The emphasis is on living in the Spirit rather than living for the pleasures of the life only.

Redeem the time

Ephesians 5: 15 See then that you walk carefully, not as fools, but as wise men, 16 making the most of the time because the days are evil. 17 Therefore do not be unwise, but understand what the will of the Lord is. 18 Do not be drunk with wine, for that is reckless living. But be filled with the Spirit. 19 Speak to one another in psalms, hymns, and spiritual songs, singing and making melody in your heart to the Lord. 20 Give thanks always for all things to God the Father in the name of our Lord Jesus Christ, 21 being submissive to one another in the fear of God.

Jesus parable of the prodigal son is often used to show God's mercy towards sinners who repent, and so it should be. I mention the story for the purposes of emphasizing what the prodigal did with his money. He squandered it. He had wine, women and song and friends who only liked him because he had money. As soon as he spent his money, he had nothing. He did not think about his future. He only lived to spend all his inheritance on riotous living.

There are many people who win the lottery of millions of dollars, but then waste it all because they are living as the prodigal. Yes, it is essential to enjoy your life, but we must plan for our futures. Being wise about making goals for our future and saving money to prepare for a home, a family, a career, the prodigal did not consider any of it.

Prodigal son –

Luke 15: 11 Then He said, "A man had two sons. 12 The younger of them said to his father, 'Father, give me the share of the property that falls to me.' So he divided his estate between them.

13 "Not many days later, the younger son gathered everything together, and journeyed to a distant country, and there squandered his possessions in prodigal living. 14 When he had spent everything, there came a severe famine in that country, and he began to be in want. 15 So he went and hired himself to a citizen of that county, who sent him into his fields to feed swine. 16 He would gladly have filled his stomach with the husks that the swine were eating, but no one gave him any.

17 "When he came to himself, he said, 'How many of my father's hired servants have an abundance of bread, and here I am perishing with hunger! 18 I will arise and go to my father, and I will say to him, "Father, I have sinned against heaven and before you. 19 I am no longer worthy to be called your son. Make me like one of your hired servants." ' 20 So he arose and came to his father.

"But while he was yet far away, his father saw him and was moved with compassion, and ran and embraced his neck and kissed him.

21 "The son said to him, 'Father, I have sinned against heaven and before you. I am no longer worthy to be called your son.'

22 "But the father said to his servants, 'Bring out the best robe and put it on him. And put a ring on his hand and shoes on his feet. 23 Bring here the fattened calf and kill it, and let us eat and be merry. 24 For this son of mine was dead, and is alive again; he was lost, and is found.' So they began to be merry.

25 "Now his older son was in the field. As he came and drew near the house, he heard music and dancing. 26 So he called one of the servants and asked what this meant. 27 He said to him, 'Your brother has come, and your father has killed the fattened calf, because he has received him safe and sound.'

The elder brother to the prodigal was jealous of the prodigal. All he did was waste all his money and come begging for mercy. He spent a fortune, but a feast was prepared for him and he was treated as royalty. The elder brother had more common sense. He stayed faithfully serving at home. He was jealous. He complained that he never even got a got to have a party with his friends. He lived in the blessings of the home. He did not understand that the prodigal had learned the wisdom of work ethic through his waste of money. He had learned that home was where he belonged.

Luke 15: 28 "He was angry and would not go in. Therefore his father came out and entreated him. 29 But he answered his father, 'Look! These many years have I served you. Nor have I ever transgressed your commands, yet never have you given me a goat, so that I might be merry with my friends. 30 But when this son of yours came, who has devoured your living with harlots, you killed the fattened calf for him.'

31 "He said to him, 'Son, you are always with me, and all that I have is yours. 32 But it was fitting to be merry and be glad, for this brother of yours was dead and is alive again; he was lost and is found.' "

Prodigal son

Jesus explained that he had not come in the word to throw out the law. He came to fulfill it. Jesus explained that whoever hates his brother is a murdered. He is naming the root sin. It is the sin that traces to Cain and Abel with Cain jealous of his brother's offering being pleasing to God and his not. He got angry and even though God warned him, he exploded in anger by murdering his brother. (Genesis 4)

1 John 3: 15 Whoever hates his brother is a murderer, and you know that no murderer has eternal life remaining in him.

Jesus Teaching About Anger Hatred

Matthew 5: 21 "You have heard that it was said by the ancients, 'You shall not murder,'[a] and 'Whoever murders shall be in danger of the judgment.' 22 But I say to you that whoever is angry with his brother without a cause shall be in danger of the judgment. And whoever says to his brother, 'Raca,' shall be in danger of the Sanhedrin. But whoever says, 'You fool,' shall be in danger of hell fire.

Jesus said that lusting in the heart was sin. |It did not eliminate the laws forbidding sex outside of marriage. He pointed to the root cause of adultery – lust. Jesus teaching is hard because it is so severe but we are to hate sin. If your eye causes you to lust do anything you can to stop it. If necessary, pluck it out. These harsh words are not literal but he uses the analogy most horrible to emphasize any playing around with sin can ensnare a person. We should have no tolerance for lust in our lives. Jesus is speaking Holy living to God for all our lives.

Jesus Speaking about Adultery

Matthew 5: 27 "You have heard that it was said by the ancients, 'You shall not commit adultery.'[c] 28 But I say to you that whoever looks on a woman to lust after her has committed adultery with her already in his heart. 29 And if your right eye causes you to sin, pluck it out and throw it away. For it is profitable that one of your members should perish, and not that your whole body be thrown into hell. 30 And if your right hand causes you to sin, cut it off and throw it away. For it is profitable for you that one of your members should perish, and not that your whole body be thrown into hell.

The Apostle speaks of consecrating your whole body, soul, spirit to God each day. Present yourself holy as a sacrifice to God each day. If we are doing it, we will most certainly be living in the Holy Spirit and living a life of self-control. We will be led by the Spirit and not the lusts of the flesh or soul.

Romans 12: 1 I urge you therefore, brothers, by the mercies of God, that you present your bodies as a living sacrifice, holy, and acceptable to God, which is your reasonable service of worship. 2 Do not be conformed to this world, but be transformed by the renewing of your mind, that you may prove what is the good and acceptable and perfect will of God.

Conclusion

Through studying the kinds of spiritual fruit in light of scripture, one can know the importance of the evidence of fruit in our lives. It is my hope and prayer that the chapters have helped you to understand scriptural importance concerning the fruit of the Spirit. Also, it is my prayer that you reader will desire to know God more intimately, placing Him first in your life, so that God may use you in your spheres of influence to shine the light of Christ brightly.

The Holy Spirit is a person who lives within believers in Jesus. The Holy Spirit teaches us, leads us and guides us and causes us to grow in godly character as well as wisdom. The gifts of the Spirit empower us to do the works of Christ but the fruit of the Spirit is the character of Christ in our lives. It is essential that when people connect with us, they sense the presence of Jesus. It can only occur if we are wholly committed to God and the promptings of the Holy Spirit.

Galatians 5: 22 But the fruit of the Spirit is love, joy, peace, patience, gentleness, goodness, faith, 23 meekness, and self-control; against such there is no law. 24 Those who are Christ's have crucified the flesh with its passions and lusts. 25 If we live in the Spirit, let us also walk in the Spirit. 26

Let us not be conceited, provoking one another and envying one another.

Should we pursue God because He is God and we are his people, we will receive strength and encouragement and transformation. Our character will be more Christ like because we will be changed in His presence from glory to glory. Communion with God means that we delight in His presence and the Holy Spirit fills us fresh. The evidence of a life living in communion with God manifests in Spiritual fruit. Our thoughts, our words and our deeds will align with God's word.

People will recognize the traits of spiritual fruit because it is unlike fleshly or evil or corrupt fruit. We will be as lights that shine because we are different than carnal people. It doesn't mean we have arrived. God will continue to transform us from glory to glory all throughout this life and in the life to come. They will know us as Christians because of the fruit of our lives.

Luke 6: 43 "A good tree does not bear corrupt fruit, nor does a corrupt tree bear good fruit. 44 Each tree is known by its own fruit. Men do not gather figs from thorns, nor do they gather grapes from a wild bush. 45 A good man out of the good treasure of his heart bears what is good, and an evil man out of the evil treasure of his heart bears what is evil. For of the abundance of the heart his mouth speaks.

Each day that you live, sincerely give yourself wholly unto God. God will fill you, empower you and use you as a vessel of honour for His glory.

1 Thessalonians 5: 23 May the very God of peace sanctify you completely. And I pray to God that your whole spirit, soul, and body be preserved blameless unto the coming of our Lord Jesus Christ. 24 Faithful is He who calls you, who also will do it.

Prayer

God thank you for the Holy Spirit. Thank you for your fruit in my life.
I pray transform me into your image. Let the fruit of the Spirit be formed in me.
Grow me in the fruit if the Spirit. Let my life be a reflection of your Spirit living in me and through me. I pray for these fruit of the Spirit.

love
joy,
peace,

patience, forbearance
gentleness, meekness
goodness,
faith,
self-control;

I yield my life to you Holy Spirit. Lead me. Be my senior partner.

PRAYERS

PRAYERS

The following prayers are samples of prayers you could pray for important reasons. You could pray the same meaning in your own words. The prayers are meant as examples only.

PRAYER FOR SALVATION

Thank you- Jesus that you died for me on the cross. Thank you that you rose from the dead and ascended into heaven. Thank you that you are coming back again. I thank you Jesus for forgiving my sins. Thank you for your blood that cleanses me from all sin and unrighteousness. Thank you that your blood makes me holy. Thank you for saving me. Fill me with the Holy Spirit to overflowing. I pray for the baptism of the Holy Spirit. Lead me to other people who love you and serve you and that can help me know more about you. Give me the discerning of spirits strong. I thank you and praise you. With my mouth, I confess Jesus Christ is my LORD. Amen.

PRAYER FOR BAPTISM OF THE HOLY SPIRIT

Thank you- Jesus that you promised to send the gift of the Holy Spirit to us. Thank you that this promise is to all believers. I am a believer. I want all of you that you will give me. I want to know you God. Baptize me in the Holy Spirit with the evidence of speaking in other tongues. I believe you want to fill me to overflowing with your Spirit so that I might be an effective witness for Christ on the earth. Thank you for saving me. Thank you for your Holy presence. [begin praising God for what He has done for you – sing worship choruses and praise God in your natural language. Believe that He is present with you – start praising and worshipping Him. As phrases come to you in other tongues, say them – praise God with new tongues.] I praise you. I thank you. I receive the baptism of the Holy Spirit.

PRAYER FOR RELEASING ANGELS

God, I thank you that angels are ministering spirits sent as ministers to us. I pray over my prayer request NAME IT HERE. God I pray release angels to perform it. I thank you for releasing the answer to me. I praise you for it. Amen.

PRAYER FOR RESISTING EVIL

I am the redeemed of the LORD. Jesus Christ has saved me. I am a new creation in Christ Jesus. Jesus blood covers me. I live in the spirit. The Holy Spirit of God fills my spirit. O Holy Spirit quicken me; give me wisdom. Pray [expecting God will give you discerning of spirits so you will have the right words to speak.]

In the name of Jesus Christ, I bind you. I rebuke you evil spirit. In the name of Jesus, I command you to go out. You have no place in my life. I cast you out. You have no place with me. I am covered by the blood of Jesus and His righteousness is my righteousness. Go out evil spirit in the name of Jesus Christ!
Thank you, Holy spirit for your holy presence. Release angels to drive out the enemy. Thank you. Amen.

PRAYER FOR PROTECTION

Holy Spirit release angels to protect me. I plead the blood of Jesus over me. I pray the protection you promise to your people. Cover me Jesus. Holy Spirit give me wisdom, discernment and understanding. Thank you for angels that guard over me. Thank you for your blood that protects me and a hedge of protection around me. I praise you O God. [praise God with some worship choruses and expect God's holy presence to be manifest in you]. Thank you. O God for protection.

PRAYER FOR HEALING

Lord Jesus, Thank you that you gave your life for me so that I can be saved, healed and delivered. I thank you for the scripture that by your stripes I am healed. I thank you for my healing.

NAME THE DISEASE I bind you in the name of Jesus. I cast you out. I pray over myself that I would be whole spirit, soul and body.

Thank you, God. for your healing manifestation in my life. I give you all the glory. Amen.

PRAYER OF REPENTENCE

Jesus, thank you for your blood shed for me. I repent of the sin of NAME IT. I thank you for liberty from sin. I cut off the root of iniquity in my family. I thank you for your empowering presence to live a Holy life. Holy Spirit lead and guide me in the paths of righteousness. Thank you for giving me godly desires. Let my life align with your word. In Jesus name. Amen.

OTHER BOOKS BY CHRIS LEGEBOW

Available on Amazon.ca Amazon.com or Kindle
Or the Create Space webstore.

Living Word Publishers

Angels: Ministering Spirits

An Excellent Spirit: Living Life Wholly Unto God

Covenant With God: God's Relationship With Man

Discovering and Using your Spiritual Gifts

Divine Healing in the Scriptures: God's Mercy Towards Man

The Commandments

The Doctrine of Christ: Essential Truths of Scripture

The Five-Fold Ministry: Gifts to the Church

Kinds of Prayer. Knowing Them and Using Them Effectively

Living Life Fully: Knowing your Purpose

Spiritual Fruit: The Importance of Godly Character

The Anointing: the Glory of God

The High Calling: Life Worth Living

The Sacraments: A Charismatic Guide

ABOUT THE AUTHOR

Chris Legebow is a Christian Professor of English and Communications. She has taught at the elementary, high school and College and University levels. She has ministered in her local churches in intercessory prayer, teaching Sunday school and other Christian Doctrine classes to children and youths. She has preached to congregations and given her testimony. Although she was not raised in a Christian home, she came to know Jesus Christ as her Saviour and LORD while she was studying in University. This radically transformed her life in terms of priorities and commitment.

She has a strong passion for the great commission – that Jesus Christ would be preached throughout all the earth believing that it a major sign of the LORD's return. She has been a part of several different types of full gospel charismatic churches but has also gained much of her insight and enlightenment from Christian Media and broadcasting. She hopes to continue ministering, serving, interceding and giving and teaching until the LORD returns.

www.ingramcontent.com/pod-product-compliance
Lightning Source LLC
Chambersburg PA
CBHW021202020426
42331CB00003B/172